AFFIRMATIVE ACTION

Other Books in the At Issue Series:

AFFIRMATIVE ACTION

Bryan J. Grapes, *Book Editor*

David L. Bender, *Publisher*
Bruno Leone, *Executive Editor*
Bonnie Szumski, *Editorial Director*
David M. Haugen, *Managing Editor*

An Opposing Viewpoints® Series

Greenhaven Press, Inc.
San Diego, California

Library of Congress Cataloging-in-Publication Data

Affirmative action / Bryan J. Grapes, book editor.
    p.   cm. — (At issue) (An opposing viewpoints series)
    Includes bibliographical references and index.
    ISBN 0-7377-0290-7 (lib. bdg. : alk. paper). —
ISBN 0-7377-0289-3 (pbk. : alk. paper)
    1. Civil rights—United States. 2. Affirmative action programs—
United States. 3. Discrimination—United States. 4. Reverse
discrimination—United States. 5. United States—Social policy.
I. Grapes, Bryan J. II. Series: At issue (San Diego, Calif.) III. Series:
Opposing viewpoints series (Unnumbered)
JC599.U5A34685   2000
331.13'3'0973—dc21   99-15925
                                                                  CIP

©2000 by Greenhaven Press, Inc., PO Box 289009,
San Diego, CA 92198-9009

Printed in the U.S.A.

Every effort has been made to trace owners of copyrighted material.

Table of Contents

Introduction

In 1996 voters in California approved the California Civil Rights Initiative (CCRI), a measure that forbids the use of race, gender, or ethnicity as criteria in state hiring or public university admissions. No longer would businesses and universities be required to adhere to affirmative action guidelines that mandated minority representation in the workforce or student body. The passage of the CCRI effectively put an end to more than thirty years of affirmative action in the state of California, and sparked a fiery debate over the continued need for affirmative action programs.

Affirmative action was part of the legislation that came out of the civil rights movement of the 1960s. It was designed by federal lawmakers to ensure that a certain percentage of African Americans (the program was later expanded to include women and other minorities) were represented in business, higher education, and government offices. When affirmative action was first introduced in the mid-1960s, it attracted little opposition. America was just emerging from the Jim Crow period, an era of racial segregation and state-supported discrimination against African Americans. Many black Americans lived in poverty, a result of centuries of slavery and racist mistreatment. The rate of unemployment in the black community was double the rate found in the white community, and inner-city neighborhoods, where many African Americans were forced to live, were saddled with substandard schools and crumbling tenement housing. Many citizens at the time felt that affirmative action was needed to address the grim conditions that plagued the black community, and open the doors of opportunity that had been previously locked to African Americans.

Today, however, many critics contend that affirmative action has outlived its usefulness. "For black people during the 1960s there was a presumption of inferiority, affirmative action was the shock treatment to change our culture," says Ward Connerly, one of the architects of the CCRI. According to Connerly, however, America is no longer the inherently racist society it was in the days of Jim Crow. Statistics cited by Stephan and Abigail Thernstrom, authors of *America in Black and White: One Nation, Indivisible,* appear to back Connerly's notion that the situation for black Americans has vastly improved. According to the Thernstroms, 40 percent of black Americans now consider themselves members of the middle class. Forty-two percent own their own homes and almost a third of the black population lives in suburbia. Because the American dream is realizable for black people today, Ward Connerly argues that "it is really hard to defend affirmative-action preferences. The only arguments you can use are either that we need diversity just for the sake of diversity, or that America is still racist. You have to embrace one of those two. And you find that you can't win those arguments at the end of the day."

Other opponents of affirmative action argue that the program was only a temporary policy meant to redress those who felt the sting of living under Jim Crow laws. Former California governor Pete Wilson contends that those who benefit from affirmative action today are granted preferential treatment "based not on past discrimination, but simply on being born into a protected group." To continue using affirmative action policies, Wilson argues, would be unfair to those who were not members of protected groups. "Even the architects of this system of special preferences never intended that it would last forever," declares Wilson. "No one, in fact, envisioned that redressing two centuries of unfairness would launch a whole new era of unfairness. But it has."

While many supporters of affirmative action concede that discrimination is not as terrible as it was during the Jim Crow period, and that the black community has made considerable economic advances, they still attest that racism and discriminatory practices have not been entirely eradicated. According to a 1998 study conducted by the Fair Housing Council in Washington, D.C., minorities are discriminated against 40 percent of the time they attempt to rent apartments or buy homes. Congressman Robert C. Scott, citing another study conducted that year by the Fair Employment Council and Urban Institute, revealed that "African-American and Latino job applicants suffer blatant and easily identifiable discrimination once in every five times they apply for a job." Furthermore, the Federal Glass Ceiling Commission reports that African-American men with a bachelor's degree earn as much as $15,180 less than their white counterparts.

Supporters of affirmative action also point to declining minority admission rates at prestigious California schools in the wake of CCRI as evidence that discrimination still exists in higher education. Of the 828 students admitted to the law school at the University of California at Berkeley in 1997, only fifteen were black. In the year prior to the implementation of the CCRI, seventy-five black students were admitted. Supporters of affirmative action argue that these numbers are proof that an admissions system based only on grades and SAT scores is culturally biased and that affirmative action programs are needed to ensure minority students a place at America's most prestigious institutes of higher learning.

Advocates of affirmative action argue that as long as racism is present in institutes of higher education and the professional world, race-conscious policies will be needed to ensure minorities a fair chance at success. They contend that the programs balance white privilege—preferential treatment granted to white people simply because they are white. "The favoritism for certain groups in the United States is so strong that it can only be remedied by actively encouraging the promotion of other groups," declares Paul Butler, an associate professor of law at the George Washington University Law School. "Specifically, favoritism for white people in the United States is such a strong, inviolable part of our country that for African Americans to have a fair chance, they have to be actively considered."

In the thirty years since the inception of affirmative action, the conditions that the programs were supposed to alleviate continue to plague the black community. According to Derrick Bell, author of *Faces at the Bottom of the Well: The Permanence of Racism*, "The unemployment rate for blacks is two and a half times the rate for whites. . . . Black per-capita income is not even two-thirds of the income for whites; and blacks . . . are three times more likely to have income below the poverty level than whites." While at the same time, a Heritage Foundation study conducted in the early 1990s indicates that the black middle class grew by more than 30 percent during the 1980s, and the ranks of black professionals increased by 75 percent. Whether or not these statistics indicate a continued need for affirmative action is the topic debated in *At Issue: Affirmative Action.*

1

Society Needs Affirmative Action

Hilary O. Shelton

Hilary O. Shelton is acting director of the Washington Bureau of the National Association for the Advancement of Colored People (NAACP).

Affirmative action programs are needed because serious discrimination still exists in American society. Without affirmative action, many promising young people will be barred from institutes of higher learning and successful careers. For example, when affirmative action was eliminated in the University of California system, black enrollment at Boalt Law School plummeted. As long as discrimination based on race and gender exists, affirmative action will be needed to ensure equal opportunity for minorities and women.

Affirmative action is necessary because discrimination is still very much a part of our country and our institutions. Some believe that equal opportunity programs such as affirmative action are no longer needed because discrimination no longer exists or because Title VII of the Civil Rights Act provides the necessary protections against discrimination.

Unfortunately, there are many misperceptions about exactly what affirmative action programs are set up to do, how they work, how successful they have been over the years, how fair they are, and how misrepresented these programs have been, both intentionally and unintentionally. Let me help address many of the myths, misunderstandings, distortions, and, in some cases, intentionally disingenuous interpretations of what affirmative action actually is and does.

What is affirmative action?

Affirmative action can be defined, in short, as any effort taken to fully integrate our society by expanding educational, employment, and contracting opportunities to the multitude of gender, ethnic, national origin, and handicapped-condition groups that have been and remain locked out of full economic, social, and/or political participation in our country.

From Hilary O. Shelton, "Affirmative Action: It's Still Needed." This article first appeared in the June 1998 issue of, and is reprinted with permission from, *The World & I*, a publication of The Washington Times Corporation; copyright ©1998.

Present-day affirmative action programs were born out of President John F. Kennedy's 1961 Executive Order 10925, which created the President's Commission on Equal Employment Opportunity.

There are scholars in the civil rights community who argue that affirmative action's roots can be traced back to the Civil War amendments. In either case, modern-day affirmative action programs based on flexible "goals and timetables" were established at a White House conference convened by President Lyndon B. Johnson shortly after the signing of the Civil Rights Act of 1964 and the Voting Rights Act of 1965.

Discriminatory practices in college admissions are locking out promising young people from professional careers and productive lives.

President Johnson convened this conference of over 300 CEOs of major U.S. corporations to pose the question, "Now that we have signed antidiscrimination provisions into our nation's laws and created safeguards to prevent voter discrimination, how do we integrate our nation's workplaces, schools, and economic institutions?" The CEOs responded in corporate business terms by recommending to the president that the nation employ common corporate practices of flexible "goals and timetables," the same effective way the business community approaches everything from "merger acquisitions" to "market takeovers."

The CEOs noted that this approach allows companies to plan ways of more fully integrating our society. In 1965, President Johnson issued Executive Order 11246 to see that this same approach was expanded to our educational institutions and our federal, state, and local contracting practices. Unfortunately, detractors of affirmative action have also distorted its meaning and principle.

Rewriting history

Opponents of affirmative action have rewritten history and clearly ignored present realities in their eagerness to eliminate present programs. They argue that affirmative action programs are no longer needed in education. They claim that the vestiges of racial and gender discrimination are dead and buried, yet the same discriminatory practices in college admissions are locking out promising young people from professional careers and productive lives.

In the late 1960s and early '70s, the NAACP and other civil rights and education organizations argued that many of our national standardized tests were "culturally discriminatory." As a result, adjustments were made to address our nation's commitment to cultural diversity based on principles of inclusion and full participation rather than segregation.

Proposition 209, the antiaffirmative action initiative that passed in California, using misleading language, abolished these advances by eliminating even the consideration of such diversity. As a result of this nouveau-segregationist, antiaffirmative action proposition, when classes began at Boalt Law School in the fall of 1998, the 270-member entering class had the same number of African Americans that the University of Mississippi had in 1962: one. A step backward to the old ways of the segregated South.

Present-day zealots focusing on eliminating affirmative action seem to flirt on the brink of a very wise man's definition of insanity. In this case, "insanity" is defined as doing the same thing over and over again yet expecting a different result. We need only compare what happens when affirmative action is eliminated, as in the aforementioned example, and how affirmative action has affected access to higher education.

In 1955, only 4.9 percent of college students ages 18–24 were African American. This figure rose to 6.5 percent during the next five years but by 1965 had slumped back to 4.9 percent. Only in the wake of affirmative action measures in the late 1960s and early '70s did the percentage of black college students begin to climb steadily: In 1970, 7.8 percent of college students were African American, in 1980, 9.1 percent, and in 1990, 11.3 percent.

Dramatic victories

The civil rights movement has clearly had its share of dramatic victories, among them *Brown v. Board of Education* and the other cases striking down segregation. Legislation such as the Civil Rights Act and the Voting Rights Act helped to advance the Constitution's promise of equal opportunity for all, including ethnic minorities, women, and others.

These judicial and legislative victories were not enough to overcome long-entrenched discrimination. One problem was that these measures frequently focused on issues of formal rights (such as the rights to vote, eat in public facilities, and sleep in public accommodations) that were particularly susceptible to judicial or statutory resolution.

In July 1970, a federal district court enjoined the state of Alabama from continuing to discriminate against African Americans in the hiring of state troopers. The court found that "in the 37-year history of the patrol, there has never been a black trooper." The order included detailed, nonnumerical provisions for assuring an end to discrimination, such as stringent controls on the civil-service certification procedure and an extensive program of recruitment of minority job applicants.

Eighteen months later, not a single African American had been hired as a state trooper, or for a civilian position connected with the state troopers. Through assertive strategies by the time the case reached the court of appeals in 1974, 25 African-American troopers and 80 African-American support personnel had been hired. Due to well-crafted affirmative action programs, the U.S. Supreme Court ultimately affirmed the orders.

In 1979, women represented only 4 percent of entry-level officers in the San Francisco Police Department. By 1985, under an affirmative action program ordered in a case in which the Department of Justice sued the city for discrimination, the number of women in the entry class had risen to 175, or 14.5 percent of the overall class.

A federal district court review of the San Francisco Fire Department in 1987 led to a consent decree that increased the number of African Americans in officer positions from 7 to 31; Hispanic officers increased from 12 to 55 and Asians from 0 to 10. Women were admitted as firefighters for the first time in the department's history.

Affirmative action is making sure that we have competent, educated leaders from and for all communities in America. Research shows that women's advancement in medical science has been accompanied by increased attention to women's health issues, such as breast and ovarian cancer, as well as expanded research in other areas.

It makes a difference

Affirmative action programs do indeed make a fundamental difference. A government study showed that women made greater gains at private companies doing business with the federal government (and therefore subject to federal affirmative action requirements) than at other companies. Female employment, in fact, rose 15.2 percent among federal contractors and only 2.2 percent elsewhere.

Affirmative action programs impel people in power to seek "merit" in untraditional places, rather than continue to make choices based on old habits, which have created a "tradition" of excluding members of certain groups.

After reading this far, you've probably realized a couple of things. First, the arguments I make sound much better than even the beginning descriptions of affirmative action outlined in the first pages of this Special Report. So obviously, many deceptions are being promoted about affirmative action.

It is often said that ethnic minorities and women receive "preferences," yet affirmative action does not require any. In matters such as college admissions, for example, women and minorities do not assume they will be treated any differently than, for example, the children of alumni or of politicians.

It is often argued that affirmative action is actually a system of hard-and-fast quotas. This is illogical. The use of quotas in hiring, contracting, and educational admissions is illegal and has been cited as such since the 1977 Supreme Court decision in *Bakke v. University of California.*

As long as there is discrimination based on race or gender, race- and gender-conscious remedies must be legally available.

The Supreme Court went further. Programs that claim to be affirmative action are also illegal if an unqualified person receives benefits over a qualified one; numerical goals are so strict that the plan lacks reasonable flexibility; the numerical goals bear no relationship to the available pool of qualified candidates and could therefore become quotas; the plan is not fixed in length; or innocent bystanders are harmed through its implementation.

Accusations of reverse discrimination are often made by those who hope to eliminate affirmative action, though evidence demonstrates that reverse discrimination is quite rare. For example, of the 91,000 employment discrimination cases before the Equal Employment Opportunity Commission, less than 2 percent are reverse discrimination cases.

Furthermore, a study conducted by Rutgers University and commissioned by the U.S. Department of Labor found that reverse discrimination is not a significant problem in employment and that a "high proportion" of claims brought by white men were "without merit." In essence, affirmative action provides employers with the largest, most diverse pool of qualified applicants from which to choose.

We have a fundamental choice about what kind of communities we want to work, earn, and live in. It is up to us to make our communities reflect our deepest American values of inclusiveness and equal opportunity for all who make up the diversity which is America. People really don't want to turn back the clock.

Affirmative action has indeed proved helpful in leveling the playing field so that all Americans can pursue the American dream. Thanks in large part to affirmative action, millions of women and men have been given an equal opportunity in education, employment, and housing.

While many private and public studies corroborate the effectiveness of affirmative action for women and minorities, numerous studies and congressional studies also show, regrettably, that serious discrimination persists in our society. Thus, we still need affirmative action. As long as there is discrimination based on race or gender, race- and gender-conscious remedies must be legally available.

2

Society Needs Affirmative Action in Higher Education

Nathan Glazer

Nathan Glazer is professor emeritus of sociology and education at Harvard University. He has written extensively on race relations, education, ethnicity, immigration, and multiculturalism. He is the author of Affirmative Discrimination, Ethnic Dilemmas, *and* We Are All Multiculturalists Now.

If test scores and grades alone were used to determine admission to top level universities, the percentage of African Americans attending major colleges or universities would drop from six percent to less than two percent. Affirmative action ensures that African American students are allowed access to prestigious universities such as Harvard and Berkeley, which have long been gateways to positions of power and influence in American society. Denying African American students access to top tier universities would undermine the value of inclusion that is vital to American democracy and send a message of despair to blacks.

The battle over affirmative action today is a contest between a clear principle on the one hand and a clear reality on the other. The principle is that ability, qualifications, and merit, independent of race, national origin, or sex, should prevail when one applies for a job or promotion, or for entry into selective institutions for higher education, or when one bids for contracts. The reality is that strict adherence to this principle would result in few African Americans getting jobs, admissions, and contracts. What makes the debate so confused is that the facts that make a compelling case for affirmative action are often obscured by the defenders of affirmative action themselves. They have resisted acknowledging how serious the gaps are between African Americans and others, how deep the preferences reach, how systematic they have become. Considerably more than a mild bent in the direction of diversity now exists, but it exists because painful facts make it necessary if blacks are to participate in more than token numbers in some key institutions of our society. The op-

Reprinted from Nathan Glazer, "In Defense of Preference," *The New Republic*, April 6, 1998, by permission of *The New Republic*; ©1998, The New Republic, Inc.

ponents of affirmative action can also be faulted: they have not fully confronted the consequences that must follow from the implementation of the principle that measured ability, qualification, merit, applied without regard to color, should be our only guide.

I argued for that principle in a 1975 book titled, provocatively, *Affirmative Discrimination.* It seemed obvious that that was what all of us, black and white, were aiming to achieve through the revolutionary civil rights legislation of the 1960s. That book dealt with affirmative action in employment, and with two other kinds of governmentally or judicially imposed "affirmative action," the equalization of the racial proportions in public schools and the integration of residential neighborhoods. I continued to argue and write regularly against governmentally required affirmative action, that is, racial preference, for the next two decades or more: it was against the spirit of the Constitution, the clear language of the civil rights acts, and the interests of all of us in the United States in achieving an integrated and just society.

It is not the unpopularity of this position in the world in which I live, liberal academia, that has led me to change my mind but, rather, developments that were unforeseen and unexpected in the wake of the successful civil rights movement. What was unforeseen and unexpected was that the gap between the educational performance of blacks and whites would persist and, in some respects, deepen despite the civil rights revolution and hugely expanded social and educational programs, that inner-city schools would continue to decline, and that the black family would unravel to a remarkable degree, contributing to social conditions for large numbers of black children far worse than those in the 1960s. In the presence of those conditions, an insistence on color-blindness means the effective exclusion today of African Americans from positions of influence, wealth, and power. It is not a prospect that any of us can contemplate with equanimity. We have to rethink affirmative action.

In a sense, it is a surprise that a fierce national debate over affirmative action has not only persisted but intensified during the Clinton years. After twelve years under two Republican presidents, Ronald Reagan and George Bush, who said they opposed affirmative action but did nothing to scale it back, the programs seemed secure. After all, affirmative action rests primarily on a presidential executive order dating back to the presidencies of Lyndon Johnson and Richard Nixon which requires "affirmative action" in employment practices from federal contractors—who include almost every large employer, university, and hospital. The legal basis for most of affirmative action could thus have been swept away, as so many noted at the time, with a "stroke of the pen" by the president. Yet two presidents who claimed to oppose affirmative action never wielded the pen.

Affirmative action and the establishment

Despite the popular majority that grumbles against affirmative action, there was (and is) no major elite constituency strongly opposed to it: neither business nor organized labor, religious leaders nor university presidents, local officials nor serious presidential candidates are to be found in opposition. Big business used to fear that affirmative action would undermine the principle of employment and promotion on the basis of qualifications. It has since become a supporter. Along with mayors and other local officials (and of course the civil rights movement), it played a key role in stopping the Reagan administration from moving against affirmative action. Most city administrations have also made their peace with affirmative action.

Two developments outside the arena of presidential politics galvanized both opponents and defenders of affirmative action. The Supreme Court changed glacially after successive Republican appointments—each of which, however, had been vetted by a Democratic Senate—and a number of circuit courts began to chip away at the edifice of affirmative action. But playing the largest role was the politically unsophisticated effort of two California professors to place on the California ballot a proposition that would insert in the California Constitution the simple and clear words, taken from the Civil Rights Act of 1964, which ban discrimination on the basis of race, national origin, or sex. The decision to launch a state constitutional proposition, Proposition 209, suddenly gave opponents the political instrument they needed to tap the majority sentiment that has always existed against preferences.

An insistence on color-blindness means the effective exclusion . . . of African Americans from positions of influence, wealth, and power.

While supporters of affirmative action do not have public opinion on their side, they do have the still-powerful civil rights movement, the major elites in education, religion, philanthropy, government, and the mass media. And their position is bolstered by a key fact: how far behind African Americans are when judged by the tests and measures that have become the common coin of American meritocracy.

The reality of this enormous gap is clearest where the tests in use are the most objective, the most reliable, and the best validated, as in the case of the various tests used for admission to selective institutions of higher education, for entry into elite occupations such as law and medicine, or for civil service jobs. These tests have been developed over many years specifically for the purpose of eliminating biases in admissions and appointments. As defenders of affirmative action often point out, paper-and-pencil tests of information, reading comprehension, vocabulary, reasoning, and the like are not perfect indicators of individual ability. But they are the best measures we have for success in college and professional schools, which, after all, require just the skills the tests measure. And the tests can clearly differentiate the literate teacher from the illiterate one or the policeman who can make out a coherent arrest report from one who cannot.

Affirmative action and education

To concentrate on the most hotly contested area of affirmative action—admission to selective institutions of higher education—and on the group in the center of the storm—African Americans: If the Scholastic Assessment

Test were used for selection in a color-blind fashion, African Americans, who today make up about six percent of the student bodies in selective colleges and universities, would drop to less than two percent, according to a 1994 study by the editor of the *Journal of Blacks in Higher Education*.

Why is this so? According to studies summarized in Stephan and Abigail Thernstrom's book, *America in Black and White*, the average combined SAT score for entering freshmen in the nation's top 25 institutions is about 1300. White applicants generally need to score a minimum of 600 on the verbal portion of the test—a score obtained by eight percent of the test-takers in 1995—and at least 650 on the mathematics section—a score obtained by seven percent of the test-takers in 1995. In contrast, only 1.7 percent of black students scored over 600 on the verbal section in 1995, and only two percent scored over 650 on the math. This represents considerable progress over the last 15 years, but black students still lag distressingly far behind their white counterparts.

There is no way of getting around this reality. Perhaps the tests are irrelevant to success in college? That cannot be sustained. They have been improved and revised over decades and predict achievement in college better than any alternative. Some of the revisions have been carried out in a near-desperate effort to exclude items which would discriminate against blacks. Some institutions have decided they will not use the tests, not because they are invalid per se, but because they pose a barrier to the increased admission of black students. Nor would emphasizing other admissions criteria, such as high school grades, make a radical difference. In any case, there is considerable value to a uniform national standard, given the enormous differences among high schools.

The banning of preference would be bad for the country.

Do qualifications at the time of admission matter? Isn't the important thing what the institutions manage to do with those they admit? If they graduate, are they not qualified? Yes, but many do not graduate. Two or three times as many African American students as white students drop out before graduation. And the tests for admission to graduate schools show the same radical disparities between blacks and others. Are there not also preferences for athletes, children of alumni, students gifted in some particular respect? Yes, but except for athletes, the disparities in academic aptitude that result from such preferences are not nearly as substantial as those which must be elided in order to reach target figures for black students. Can we not substitute for the tests other factors—such as the poverty and other hardships students have overcome to reach the point of applying to college? This might keep up the number of African Americans, but not by much, if the studies are to be believed. A good number of white and Asian applicants would also benefit from such "class-based" affirmative action.

(I have focused on the effect of affirmative action—and its possible abolition—on African Americans. But, of course, there are other beneficiaries. Through bureaucratic mindlessness, Asian Americans and Hispanics were also given affirmative action. But Asian Americans scarcely need it. Major groups—not all—of Hispanic Americans trail behind whites but mostly for reasons we understand: problems with the English language and the effect on immigrant children of the poor educational and economic status of their parents. We expect these to improve in time as they always have with immigrants to the United States. And, when it comes to women, there is simply no issue today when it comes to qualifying in equal numbers for selective institutions of higher and professional education.)

How, then, should we respond to this undeniable reality? The opponents of affirmative action say, "Let standards prevail whatever the result." So what if black students are reduced to two percent of our selective and elite student bodies? Those who gain entry will know that they are properly qualified for entry, that they have been selected without discrimination, and their classmates will know it too. The result will actually be improved race relations and a continuance of the improvements we have seen in black performance in recent decades. Fifteen years from now, perhaps three or four percent of students in the top schools will be black. Until then, blacks can go to less competitive institutions of higher education, perhaps gaining greater advantage from their education in so doing. And, meanwhile, let us improve elementary and high school education—as we have been trying to do for the last 15 years or more.

Yet we cannot be quite so cavalier about the impact on public opinion—black and white—of a radical reduction in the number of black students at the Harvards, the Berkeleys, and the Amhersts. These institutions have become, for better or worse, the gateways to prominence, privilege, wealth, and power in American society. To admit blacks under affirmative action no doubt undermines the American meritocracy, but to exclude blacks from them by abolishing affirmative action would undermine the legitimacy of American democracy.

My argument is rooted in history. African Americans—and the struggle for their full and fair inclusion in U.S. society—have been a part of American history from the beginning. Our Constitution took special—but grossly unfair—account of their status, our greatest war was fought over their status, and our most important constitutional amendments were adopted because of the need to right past wrongs done to them. And, amid the civil rights revolution of the 1960s, affirmative action was instituted to compensate for the damage done to black achievement and life chances by almost 400 years of slavery, followed by state-sanctioned discrimination and massive prejudice.

Persistent differences

Yet, today, a vast gulf of difference persists between the educational and occupational status of blacks and whites, a gulf that encompasses statistical measures of wealth, residential segregation, and social relationships with other Americans. Thirty years ago, with the passage of the great civil rights laws, one could have reasonably expected—as I did—that all would be set right by now. But today, even after taking account of substantial progress and change, it is borne upon us how continuous, rooted, and substantial the differences between African Americans and other Americans remain.

The judgment of the elites who support affirmative action—the college presidents and trustees, the religious leaders, the corporate executives—and the judgment even of many of those who oppose it but hesitate to act against it—the Republican leaders in Congress, for example—is that the banning of preference would be bad for the country. I agree. Not that everyone's motives are entirely admirable; many conservative congressmen, for example, are simply afraid of being portrayed as racists even if their opposition to affirmative action is based on a sincere desire to support meritocratic principle. The college presidents who support affirmative action, under the fashionable mantra of diversity, also undoubtedly fear the student demonstrations that would occur if they were to speak out against preferences.

But there are also good-faith motives in this stand, and there is something behind the argument for diversity. What kind of institutions of higher education would we have if blacks suddenly dropped from six or seven percent of enrollment to one or two percent? The presence of blacks, in classes in social studies and the humanities, immediately introduces another tone, another range of questions (often to the discomfort of black students who do not want this representational burden placed upon them). The tone may be one of embarrassment and hesitation and self-censorship among whites (students and faculty). But must we not all learn how to face these questions together with our fellow citizens? We should not be able to escape from this embarrassment by the reduction of black students to minuscule numbers.

The weakness in the "diversity" defense is that college presidents are not much worried about the diversity that white working-class kids, or students of Italian or Slavic background, have to offer. Still, there is a reputable reason for that apparent discrepancy. It is that the varied ethnic and racial groups in the United States do not, to the same extent as African Americans, pose a test of the fairness of American institutions. These other groups have not been subjected to the same degree of persecution or exclusion. Their status is not, as the social status of African Americans is, the most enduring reproach to the egalitarian ideals of American society. And these other groups have made progress historically, and make progress today, at a rate that incorporates them into American society quickly compared to blacks.

A flawed critique

This is the principal flaw in the critique of affirmative action. The critics are defending a vitally important principle, indeed, the one that should be the governing principle of institutions of higher education: academic competence as the sole test for distinguishing among applicants and students. This principle, which was fought for so energetically during the 1940s and 1950s through laws banning discrimination in admission on the basis of race, national origin, or religion, should not be put aside lightly. But, at present, it would mean the near exclusion from our best educational institutions of a group that makes up twelve percent of the population. In time, I am convinced, this preference will not be needed. Our laws and customs and our primary and secondary educational systems will fully incorporate black Americans into American society, as other disadvantaged groups have been incorporated. The positive trends of recent decades will continue. But we are still, though less than in the past, "two nations," and one of the nations cannot be excluded so thoroughly from institutions that confer access to the positions of greatest prestige and power.

On what basis can we justify violating the principle that measured criteria of merit should govern admission to selective institutions of higher education today? It is of some significance to begin with that we in the United States have always been looser in this respect than more examination-bound systems of higher education in, say, Western Europe: we have always left room for a large degree of freedom for institutions of higher education, public as well as private, to admit students based on nonacademic criteria. But I believe the main reasons we have to continue racial preferences for blacks are, first, because this country has a special obligation to blacks that has not been fully discharged, and second, because strict application of the principle of qualification would send a message of despair to many blacks, a message that the nation is indifferent to their difficulties and problems.

Strict application of the principle of qualification would send a message . . . to many blacks . . . that the nation is indifferent to their difficulties and problems.

Many, including leading black advocates of eliminating preference, say no: the message would be, "Work harder and you can do it." Well, now that affirmative action is becoming a thing of the past in the public colleges and universities of California and Texas, we will have a chance to find out. Yet I wonder whether the message of affirmative action to black students today really ever has been, "Don't work hard; it doesn't matter for you because you're black; you will make it into college anyway." Colleges are indeed looking for black students, but they are also looking for some minimal degree of academic effort and accomplishment, and it is a rare ambitious African American student seeking college entry who relaxes because he believes his grades won't matter at all.

One of the chief arguments against racial preference in college and professional school admissions is that more blacks will drop out, the quality of blacks who complete the courses of instruction will be inferior, and they will make poorer lawyers, doctors, or businessmen. Dropping out is common in American higher education and does not necessarily mean that one's attendance was a total loss. Still, the average lower degree of academic performance has, and will continue to have, effects even for the successful: fewer graduating black doctors will go into research; more will go into practice and administration. More blacks in business corporations will be in personnel. Fewer graduating black lawyers will go into corporate law firms; more will work for government.

And more will become judges, because of another and less disputed form of affirmative action, politics. Few protest at the high number of black magistrates in cities with large black populations—we do not appoint judges by examination. Nor do we find it odd or objectionable that Democratic presidents will appoint more black lawyers as judges, or that even a Republican president will be sure to appoint one black Supreme Court justice. What is at work here is the principle of participation. It is a more legitimate principle in politics and government than it is for admission to selective institutions of higher education. But these are also gateways to power, and the principle of participation cannot be flatly ruled out for them.

Self-imposed affirmative action

Whatever the case one may make in general for affirmative action, many difficult issues remain: What kind, to what extent, how long, imposed by whom, by what decision-making process? It is important to bear in mind that affirmative action in higher education admissions is, for the most part, a policy that has been chosen (albeit sometimes under political pressure) by the institutions themselves. There are racial goals and targets for employment and promotion for all government contractors, including colleges and universities, set by government fiat, but targets on student admissions are not imposed by government, except for a few traditionally black or white institutions in the South.

Let us preserve this institutional autonomy. Just as I would resist governmentally imposed requirements that these institutions meet quotas of black admissions, so would I also oppose a judicial or legislative ban on the use of race in making decisions on admission. Ballot measures like Proposition 209 are more understandable given the abuses so common in systems of racial preference. But it is revealing that so many other states appear to have had second thoughts and that the California vote is therefore not likely to be repeated. (A report in the *Chronicle of Higher Education* was headlined "LEGISLATURES SHOW LITTLE ENTHUSIASM FOR MEASURES TO END RACIAL PREFERENCES"; in this respect, the states are not unlike Congress.)

We should retain the freedom of institutions of higher and professional education to make these determinations for themselves. As we know, they would almost all make room for a larger percentage of black students than would otherwise qualify. This is what these institutions do today. They defend what they do with the argument that diversity is a good thing. I think what they really mean is that a large segment of the American population, significant not only demographically but historically and politically and morally, cannot be so thoroughly excluded. I agree with them.

I have discussed affirmative action only in the context of academic admissions policy. Other areas raise other questions, other problems. And, even in this one area of college and university admissions, affirmative action is not a simple and clear and uncomplicated solution. It can be implemented wisely or foolishly, and it is often done foolishly, as when college presidents make promises to protesting students that they cannot fulfill, or when institutions reach too far below their minimal standards with deleterious results for the academic success of the students they admit, for their grading practices, and for the legitimacy of the degrees they offer. No matter how affirmative action in admissions is dealt with, other issues remain or will emerge. More black students, for example, mean demands for more black faculty and administrators and for more black-oriented courses. Preference is no final answer (just as the elimination of preference is no final answer). It is rather what is necessary to respond to the reality that, for some years to come, yes, we are still two nations, and both nations must participate in the society to some reasonable degree.

Fortunately, those two nations, by and large, want to become more united. The United States is not Canada or Bosnia, Lebanon or Malaysia. But, for the foreseeable future, the strict use of certain generally reasonable tests as a benchmark criterion for admissions would mean the de facto exclusion of one of the two nations from a key institutional system of the society, higher education. Higher education's governing principle is qualification—merit. Should it make room for another and quite different principle, equal participation? The latter should never become dominant. Racial proportional representation would be a disaster. But basically the answer is yes—the principle of equal participation can and should be given some role. This decision has costs. But the alternative is too grim to contemplate.

3

Affirmative Action Promotes Diversity

Chang-Lin Tien

Chang-Lin Tien is a professor of mechanical engineering at the University of California at Berkeley and served as the university's chancellor from 1990 to 1997.

Affirmative action programs have fostered an atmosphere of diversity and racial tolerance on college campuses across America. Students who are taught in a culturally diverse setting are better equipped to succeed in a multicultural and multiracial society. Because it promotes interaction between people of different races, affirmative action can be an effective tool in bridging racial divisions.

When the debate over affirmative action in higher education exploded, my open support surprised many. My personal view about using race, ethnicity, and sex among the factors in student admissions has put me at odds with many, including the majority of the Regents of the University of California who govern my campus.

With California voters having decided in November, 1996, to end all state-sponsored affirmative action programs, silence would seem to be a far more prudent course for me to take. Educators already have enough battles to fight—declining public funding, controversy over the national research agenda, and eroding public support for America's academic mission.

Why did I take on the explosive issue of affirmative action? My participation in the debate is inspired both by my role in higher education and my experience as an immigrant of Chinese descent. As chancellor of the University of California, Berkeley, I had seen the promise of affirmative action come true. Today, no ethnic or racial group constitutes a majority among the university's 21,000 undergraduates. Berkeley students enter better prepared and graduate at the highest rate in our history. Through daily interaction in classrooms, laboratories, and residence halls, they develop a deep understanding of different cultures and outlooks.

As an immigrant, I know the U.S. is the land of opportunity. Unlike any other nation in history, America has taken pride in being built by im-

Reprinted from Chang-Lin Tien, "In Defense of Affirmative Action," *USA Today* magazine, November 1997, with permission. Copyright ©1997 by the Society for the Advancement of Education.

migrants and allows foreign-born people like me to participate in the world's greatest democracy.

Racial division

In 1956, I came here for graduate studies, a virtually penniless immigrant from China with a limited grasp of the language and customs of the U.S. A teaching fellowship was my income. To stretch my frugal budget, I walked across town to eat at the least expensive restaurants and scouted out the lowest-cost washing machines and dryers.

As a result of the wonderful educational opportunities I have enjoyed, I have contributed to America. My research in heat transfer has enhanced our engineering expertise in many critical technologies, including nuclear reactor safety, space shuttle thermal design, and electronic systems cooling. My former students teach and conduct research in America's top universities and industries. I was privileged to head the university with the largest number and highest percentage of top-ranked doctoral programs in the nation.

Yet, along with opportunity, I have encountered the harsh realities of racial discrimination that are part of America's legacy. Like it or not, this history of racial division is linked with the debate over affirmative action. Although the U.S. has made great strides, race still divides our society. It is part of the debate over how we afford equal opportunities to everyone.

My first months in the U.S. reflect how opportunity and racial intolerance can be linked. I served as a teaching fellow for a professor who refused to pronounce my name and only referred to me as "Chinaman." One day, the professor directed me to adjust some valves in a large laboratory apparatus. When I climbed a ladder, I lost my balance and instinctively grabbed a nearby steam pipe. It was so hot, it produced a jolt of pain that nearly caused me to faint, but I did not scream out. I stuffed my throbbing hand into my coat pocket and waited until the class ended. Then I ran to the hospital emergency room, where I was treated for a burn that completely had singed the skin off my palm.

My response seems to fit the Asian model minority myth: Say nothing and go about your business. My silence had nothing to do with stoicism, though. I simply did not want to endure the humiliation of having the professor scold me in front of the class.

Today, after four decades of major civil rights advances, members of racial and ethnic minorities like me no longer are intimidated into silence. Still, serious racial divisions remain. Those of us who are of Asian, Latino, or Middle Eastern heritage have become accustomed to having passersby tell us, "Go back to your own country." More typical is the polite query: "What country do you come from?" It makes no difference if you are first-generation or fifth-generation. If you have Asian, Latino, or Middle Eastern features or surname, many Americans assume you were born in another country. The ancestors of a professor in the university's School of Optometry left China to work in California during the 1850s. Even though his roots run far deeper than those of the vast majority of Californians, people invariably ask him where he was born.

Our nation can not afford to ignore the racial strife that continues to divide America. Nor should we forget that the U.S. is a great democracy built by diverse peoples. It is critical to attack the problem of racial division and build on national strengths. The finest hope for meeting this challenge will be America's colleges and universities.

These institutions launched affirmative admissions programs to open their doors to promising minority students who lacked educational and social opportunities. Over time, the composition of America's college students has changed. Campuses are more diverse than at any time in history.

Critics of continuing race or ethnicity as a consideration in student admissions argue that affirmative action unfairly discriminates against white and Asian-American applicants who worked hard in high school and received top grades. They further maintain that it no longer is needed to provide opportunities. Although I agree that affirmative action is a temporary measure, the time has not yet come to eliminate it. Educational opportunities vary dramatically in U.S. public schools.

The inner-city student can find illegal drugs more readily than computer labs and after-school enrichment courses. In contrast, the more affluent suburban student is hooked into the Internet, enrolled in honor classes, and looking forward to summer instruction.

Students on campuses that lack diversity can gain just a limited . . . understanding of the challenges and opportunities in a highly diverse nation.

Given this reality, it is fair and equitable to consider race and ethnicity as one factor among many—including test scores and grade-point averages—in admitting qualified youths to highly competitive universities. Such an approach remains the most effective way to make sure America does not turn into a two-tiered society of permanent haves and have-nots.

Assisting promising students is not the only reason for preserving affirmative action. The diversity of students, faculty, and staff that it inspired is one of the most exciting and challenging phenomena in American higher education today. All students stand to gain, whether they are whites, Asian-Americans, or traditionally underrepresented minorities.

I believe students on campuses that lack diversity can gain just a limited, theoretical understanding of the challenges and opportunities in a highly diverse nation. A lecture on Toni Morrison's novels or the theater of Luis Valdez is not enough.

No career or profession will be untouched by the rapid sociodemographic change. For instance, consider how America's diversity will affect those in U.S. colleges and universities. Education students will teach many youngsters born in different countries. Medical students will treat many patients with beliefs and attitudes about medicine that differ from the Western outlook. Students of engineering and business will work for major corporations, where they will be expected to design, develop, and market products that sell not just in the U.S., but in markets around the world. Law students will represent clients whose experience with the judicial system in their neighborhoods and barrios is distinctive from the way middle America regards the law.

A matter of diversity

Diversity in colleges and universities benefits all students, not just the underrepresented minorities. Our experience at Berkeley shows the promise of affirmative action. Every time I walk across campus, I am impressed by the vibrant spirit of our diverse community. Nowhere do you see this better than teeming Sproul Plaza, where dozens of student groups set up tables representing a wide range of social, political, ethnic, and religious interests.

At Berkeley, undergraduates are about 40% Asian-American; 31% non-Hispanic Caucasian; 14% Hispanic; six percent African-American; and one percent Native American, with the rest undeclared. About one-quarter of freshmen come from families earning $28,600 a year or less; another quarter from families that earn more than $90,000. The median family income reported for 1994 freshmen was $58,000.

Young people from barrios, comfortable suburbs, farm towns, and the inner city come together at Berkeley to live and study side by side. Not surprisingly, they find first-time interactions with students from different backgrounds occasionally fraught with misunderstanding and tension.

As chancellor, I made it a point to listen and talk with students. [The] casual conversations [I had] as I walked the campus to meetings, dropping in at the library after work, and sitting in on classes gave me greater insight into the day-to-day lives of Berkeley students. They told me about the practical challenges of moving beyond the stereotypes and learning to respect differences.

Some African-Americans and Latinos confided they sometimes believed their professors and white classmates considered them to be inferior academically. This made them feel isolated from the general campus community. Some whites told me they felt like they had been pushed out by less-deserving blacks and Latinos. They also believed that overachieving Asians were depriving them of educational opportunities.

The views of Asian-Americans differed. Some were disturbed by the "model minority" stereotype. They complained that it pits them against other minorities and masks the problem of discrimination they still face. Others were concerned about issues such as affirmative action. They believed it is fair to base admissions on academic qualifications alone—which would open the door to more Asian-Americans.

Diversity in colleges and universities benefits all students.

These differing outlooks are not cause for alarm. Instead, they reflect the views held in society at large. It is important that students of all racial and ethnic groups told me they valued the opportunities on our campus to come together with people of diverse backgrounds. I believe it is this attitude our campus must reinforce as we help them to address differences.

The residence halls are the first place students come together. Because we understand the challenges associated with living together with those who have different values and outlooks, we run programs that encourage students to discuss racial and cultural differences openly.

Our campus tradition of academic freedom is critical. When issues arise where students are divided by race, they don't ignore the matter. We encourage all members of the campus community to air differences freely in forums, seminars, and rallies. Whether the topic is affirmative action, enforcement of the successful California ballot measure that would ban illegal immigrants from public schools, or the organization of ethnic studies, students and faculty passionately debate the pros and cons.

Let me cite an example. In 1995, the longstanding conflict between Israelis and Palestinians led to fiery exchanges between Jewish and Muslim students on our campus. During rallies and counter-protests, an Israeli flag was ripped apart, while Muslim students alleged they were being demonized.

We addressed the issues directly. The campus held meetings to denounce "hate speech," while open debate was encouraged. My top objective was to make sure that discussions on this charged issue did not degenerate into racial epithets. I decided to forego an invitation from President Bill Clinton to attend a White House meeting so I could meet with students who were central to the debate and help them hammer out their differences.

It is this tradition of study and debate that makes American higher education so valuable. Colleges and universities are a haven for open discussion. Only by addressing differences directly can students reach a deeper understanding of the real meaning of diversity.

Maintaining diversity

Today, our campus faces a major new challenge. The University of California Regents have voted to end the use of race, ethnicity, and sex as a factor among many others in student admissions at its nine campuses in 1998. At first, the Regents' decision stunned me. I questioned whether we could preserve the diversity which is so important to our campus after losing an important tool for achieving student enrollments that reflect California's wide-ranging population.

Yet, I quickly realized the importance of the Regents' reaffirmation of their commitment to diversity even though they discarded affirmative action. So, I decided to take the Chinese approach to challenge. In Chinese, the character for crisis actually is two characters: One stands for danger and the other for opportunity. For me, times of crisis present both challenges and opportunities.

The end of affirmative action at the University of California gave us the impetus for trying new approaches to improving the eligibility rates of high school students traditionally underrepresented in higher education. At Berkeley, we set to work right away to turn challenge into opportunity. We realized our efforts would be doomed unless we worked even more closely with the public schools. Within weeks of the affirmative action decision, I joined the superintendents of the San Francisco Bay Area's major urban school districts to announce our new campaign to diversity: The Berkeley Pledge.

The announcement made it clear that our campus would not shirk its commitment to diversity. Instead, we pledged to step up the drive to support the efforts of disadvantaged youth to qualify for admission and preserve access to higher education. I committed $1,000,000 from private gifts, and we are seeking additional private support to fund this innovative approach.

America has come a long way since the days of Jim Crow segregation. It would be a tragedy if our nation's colleges and universities slipped backward, denying access to talented, but disadvantaged, youth and eroding the diversity that helps to prepare the leaders of the 21st century.

I find one aspect of the debate over affirmative action to be especially disturbing. There seems to be an underlying assumption that if it is eliminated, the nation will have solved the problems associated with racial division. Nothing could be further from the truth. It is critical for America to address the issue of how people from diverse backgrounds are going to study, work, and live in the same neighborhoods together in harmony, not strife.

This is the challenge in higher education. It demands the collaboration of students, faculty, staff, and alumni at universities and colleges across America. All must work together to maintain the diversity that is essential to excellence.

4

Affirmative Action Benefits the Workplace and Economy

James A. Buford Jr.

James A. Buford Jr. is a management consultant and a professor in the College of Business at Auburn University.

Though discrimination is not as rampant as it was in the past, minorities and women are still underrepresented in many types of jobs. Affirmative action programs ensure that qualified minorities and women are included in the pool of potential candidates for skilled positions. The failure to hire talented women and minorities is a poor use of human resources, and will ultimately harm the workplace and the national economy.

You will, of course, wish to know my credentials for presenting a conservative case for affirmative action in employment. Well, first, as a social scientist with the requisite degrees and academic publications, I am licensed to diagnose the ills of the American workplace from my seat in the ivory tower. But I am also a management consultant with clients who often call on me to prepare their cases in fair-employment disputes, testify as an expert witness, and provide other services adversarial to plaintiffs claiming they have suffered discrimination. My politics are conservative and I have a strong Republican voting record. I live in Alabama, a state that takes a dim view of social engineering. I hold a professorship in the College of Business at Auburn University, not exactly a hotbed of liberal thinking. All this may give me an insider advantage in disputing the conventional wisdom of the Right, but my actual views on the issue at hand probably won't bring me an invitation to work on the civil rights platform plank at the next Republican convention.

Apart from abortion, affirmative action is arguably the most loaded political issue of the day, and the least rationally argued. What passes for debate is mainly the clash of opposing evangelists with messages full of sound bites, catch phrases, and code words preaching disinformation to choirs of true believers. One choir gets the message: "Because you are black or female you are a victim and we are going to make them give you

Reprinted from James A. Buford Jr., "Affirmative Action Works," *Commonweal*, June 19, 1998, by permission of *Commonweal*.

a job." The other choir hears: "They want to take away your job and give it to a black, or a female, or a black female." My effort will be to examine the facts and the arguments on the way to my conclusion, which is that affirmative action works rather well, at least in the context of employment. The points I will make apply less, if at all, to other race-conscious initiatives that carry this label.

A level playing field

Let's begin with the metaphor of the playing field. One argument is that the field was leveled in 1964 with the passage of Title VII of the Civil Rights Act. Or that, with more than thirty years of enforcement, it must be level by now. Well, it really is more level than it was. The mainly liberal view that equal employment opportunity somehow ended with the presidency of Ronald Reagan and that the Republicans spent twelve years turning back the clock is simply wrong. Republican presidents since Richard Nixon tended to be much more progressive on this issue than they were ever able to admit to their followers on the right. Most overt discrimination against blacks has ended. Systemic or unintentional discrimination resulting from seemingly neutral hiring practices, such as employment tests that commonly had an adverse effect on black applicants, were addressed by the 1971 Supreme Court decision in *Griggs v. Duke Power Company.*

Nevertheless, minorities and females continue to be underrepresented in many types of jobs and concentrated in others. For example, most of a company's accountants may be white and most of its custodians black. That may be because the company recruits for entry-level accounting jobs at colleges and universities where enrollment is predominantly white. Perhaps the company relies on employee referrals (the old-boy network). Another explanation has to do with how decisions are made when a pool of applicants includes both blacks and whites and it is necessary to select those who are "best qualified." A hiring decision is ultimately a judgment call made after a job interview by managers and supervisors with preconceived ideas about the attributes a candidate should have—attributes usually similar to their own. Although job interviews are a well-established management prerogative, research has shown that they are notoriously unreliable predictors of successful choices. Even at entry level, most individuals who make hiring decisions are white males; the higher the job level, the more this is likely to be the case. In the typical "multiple hurdle" hiring process, all the applicants who make it to the final pool are "qualified," and this group often includes minorities and women. Some do get hired, of course, and probably some are selected because they are black or female. In the aggregate, however, hiring officials tend to follow their instincts, and even in the absence of ill will or bias this works to the disadvantage of minorities and women. I have observed this pattern in my consulting practice, which, I should add, is not limited to the South. There are other factors that help to explain the underrepresentation of minorities and women in certain jobs, and sorting them out would be very difficult. But to say that discrimination is not part of the problem is about as credible as saying that it explains everything.

There are, of course, remedies for discrimination. An applicant who has been discriminated against can file a charge with the Equal Employment Opportunity Commission (EEOC). Even if the EEOC finds for the complainant, however, the agency cannot enforce its ruling but must take the case to federal court. Very few such cases are actually litigated by the EEOC; usually, the charging party is given a private right to sue. But the process is expensive and proving intentional discrimination is difficult. The employer need only state a "legitimate, nondiscriminatory reason" for the decision—for example, that a black applicant for an accountant position had less experience than a white applicant. Once the plaintiff would have been able to prevail—and to receive appropriate relief, including a job placement, back pay, and possible punitive and compensatory damages—by showing that the white applicant did not have more experience. But since the Supreme Court decision in *St. Mary's Honor Center v. Hicks* (1993), the plaintiff has been required to prove that the reason was a "pretext for discrimination"; he or she must uncover a prejudicial statement made by a hiring official, or a similar "smoking gun." That might have happened thirty years ago but today most employers are sophisticated enough to avoid doing or saying things that would expose them to legal risk.

[Affirmative action] most certainly does not impose gender and racial preferences or quotas.

But does this justify laws and regulations requiring employers to hire people because of their race or gender to meet quotas, thereby bringing about reverse discrimination—as was suggested in TV spots used by the Jesse Helms campaign in the 1996 Senate campaign in North Carolina? That does seem unfair, and apparently enough voters agreed to re-elect Senator Helms. Maybe such laws and regulations should be repealed outright, or, as President Bill Clinton has suggested, at least be fixed.

The Civil Rights Act

So let's look, beginning with Title VII of the Civil Rights Act as amended. The part on racial quotas is in 703(j), which says: "[No employer is required] to grant preferential treatment to any individual or group because of the race, color, religion, sex, or national origin of such individual or group on account of an imbalance that may exist. . . ." And legislation passed in 1991 discourages employers from using any such practices. No quotas here. So perhaps the problem rises not out of statutes but from regulations. Presidential Executive Order 11246, issued by Lyndon Johnson in 1965, established the Office of Federal Contract Compliance Programs, which requires employers with government contracts—a category that includes most major corporations as well as many small businesses, banks and other financial institutions, and colleges and universities—to have affirmative-action programs. That the order originated with LBJ definitely raises a flag for conservatives. But it was also signed by Richard Nixon, Gerald Ford, Ronald Reagan, and George Bush, who was so adamant about not having quotas one had only to read his lips.

Did these presidents fail to read what they were signing? Or did they actually read the order and decide it was reasonable? Perhaps they conferred with employer groups—overwhelmingly conservative and Republican—and learned that the business community was generally supportive. That, in fact, is how it happened. Furthermore, the order does not require preferential treatment or quotas. Rather, it requires covered employers to compare utilization of minorities and women in various job groups in their work force with the availability of qualified minorities and women in the relevant labor market. The key words here are "availability" and "qualified." That 35 percent of a given population is black does not mean that all of the blacks are qualified to be accountants. Availability would consider the percentage of blacks in the population but focus mainly on the component of that percentage qualified for a particular job. Where underutilization is found, employers are required to set goals and "use all reasonable efforts" to hire qualified minorities and women. Employers are allowed to establish these goals based on their own determination of availability.

Assume, for example, that a federal contractor has fifty accountants, of whom only two, or 4 percent, are black. The employer analyzes the relevant labor market and determines that the availability of qualified blacks is 10 percent. If ten accountants are to be hired this year, the employer would set a goal equal to availability, and attempt to hire one black applicant. In subsequent years, three more black accountants will be hired and underutilization will no longer exist in this job category with this employer. At this juncture, devotees of the level-playing-field metaphor might again make their point: that if affirmative action was ever necessary, it isn't necessary now. They're right—and that very same executive order anticipates their argument. Once the goal has been reached, the employer is no longer required—in fact, is not allowed—to set goals for hiring black accountants.

Some employers with no government contracts nevertheless adopt voluntary affirmative action plans. Underutilization of women and minorities exposes an employer to legal liability under the disparate impact theory of discrimination established by the *Griggs* decision. If a group of plaintiffs can identify hiring practices which appear to screen out blacks at a disproportionate rate, the burden is on the employer to justify those practices. In 1989, the Supreme Court decision in *Wards Cove Packing Co. v. Antonio* modified the case law, making it somewhat more difficult for plaintiffs to sue under the disparate impact theory, but Congress then enacted *Griggs* into the Civil Rights Act of 1991, signed by President Bush.

It is not good for the country when qualified women and minorities are underrepresented in many types of jobs.

Doesn't this open the door to potential abuse? What about employers fearful of getting sued and therefore rushing to get their numbers up? There are probably some private employers who are sympathetic toward minorities and who want to be socially responsible. And, of course, the public sector is full of bleeding heart liberals. Won't both the supercautious and the hyperliberal go overboard in the direction of reverse discrimination?

No doubt some do, but such informal, ad hoc affirmative action is recognized and forbidden in case law. In *Daugherty v. Barry*, for example, a U.S. District Court ruled that the District of Columbia violated Title VII when eight eligible white applicants were bypassed in favor of two black applicants. The court found that the hiring decision was based on the city administrator's "personal vision" rather than a properly set goal. Not only case law but also federal regulations covering voluntary affirmative-action plans establish procedural safeguards—prohibiting, for example, laying off whites to maintain a racial balance or refusing to hire qualified white males—provisions very similar to those applying to government contractors.

Finally, in particular cases federal courts may require employers to adopt affirmative-action plans until they achieve compliance. In 1971 the Alabama Department of Public Safety had not been able to find even one black applicant qualified to be a state trooper, a problem that a federal judge solved by imposing an affirmative-action plan under which the judge determined availability, established goals, and instructed the department not merely to "use all reasonable efforts" but to "find and hire" qualified black applicants. Court-ordered plans imposed when discrimination is found to be pervasive and egregious can be much more stringent than voluntary plans or those required by executive order, but they are still designed to end when goals are met. Such cases are rare today, and most of the early orders have been vacated.

A mildly proactive approach

With the possible exception of this last category, it will be seen that affirmative action amounts to little more than a mildly proactive approach to equal employment opportunity. It most certainly does not impose gender and racial preferences or quotas, as its opponents would have us believe, nor does it go as far as its supporters would probably like. True, it is obviously not color-blind or gender-blind. Moreover, a basic tenet of conservative orthodoxy warns against being even mildly proactive; in the neoclassical school of economics (the one we attended), market forces are considered the appropriate means of dealing with social questions.

But the doctrine of market efficacy assumes free mobility of resources: Capital (equity or debt funding) flows to the enterprise where the return is highest, the latest technology is used, and human resources are deployed where their skills match the tasks to be performed. The underrepresentation of qualified minorities and women in certain jobs reveals a barrier to the mobility of human resources. Some neoclassicists would argue that an imperfect market is better than a governmentally regulated market; firms that do not hire the best-qualified workers of any race or sex will suffer, much as they would if they acquired too much debt load or chose the wrong accounting software. In the long run it all works out. But, as John Maynard Keynes (admittedly not a neoclassicist) once pointed out, in the long run we are all dead. Moreover, discrimination in hiring imposes costs not only on individuals but on society; if human resources are not put to their highest and best use, the economy performs less well and expenditures for social services and income maintenance rise; and this violates another neoclassicist assumption, which holds that in a true market economy enterprises pay all the costs of production and do not shift them to society. To the extent that affirmative action matches up minorities and women with jobs for which they are qualified and are as likely as not to be "best qualified," the cost to the enterprise (and to the economy) becomes much smaller and in some cases disappears entirely. Perhaps conservatives should also ponder the possibility that that black accountant may find a better software package for the company's financial information system, receive a generous increase in salary, and become a Republican favoring more and better tax breaks for corporations.

More basically: As a conservative I recognize an obligation to support programs that promote personal responsibility and join opportunity with merit. That sounds a lot like what those people who conceived the "Contract with America" had in mind. If we expect people to buy into the work ethic, we might want to take steps to ensure that that attitude is rewarded. It is not good for an accountant always to be called and never to be chosen. It is not good for a welfare mother who has just completed a clerical-skills training program not to be able to find a job as a secretary. It is not good for the country when qualified women and minorities are underrepresented in many types of jobs.

Affirmative action works

Finally, again as a conservative I recognize an obligation to support programs that work as they are supposed to. And affirmative-action programs actually do work. That's especially true of those established by government contractors under the executive order. But many employers undertake this process on their own; in my consulting work I have observed the operation of such plans for a number of years, and the result has been a substantial increase in the numbers of both minorities and women in jobs that few or none could have obtained earlier. Of course there have been problems with affirmative action, but these tend to be the overdramatized exceptions that make it into TV spots. For the most part, affirmative action has escaped the unintended consequences that plague many social programs, and the progress has come without a great deal of bureaucratic complexity, without imposing unnecessary burdens of time and cost on employers, without creating barriers to employment of white males, and without creating ill will.

In the community of employment managers, testing professionals, attorneys, consultants, and academics who deal with affirmative action, I would expect to find some areas of disagreement with what I have argued, but most would agree that I have made a legitimate case. Why, then, do political leaders and commentators on both sides insist on making affirmative action into an issue like abortion, where the policy options represent fundamental philosophical differences and irreconcilable policy choices? Affirmative action is not a zero-sum game, and its merit does not depend on axioms of political correctness, liberal variety. Maybe we conservatives should actually embrace affirmative action as one of those rare government programs that further our agenda. How about a statement in "The Contract with America, Part II"?

5

Affirmative Action Balances White Privilege

Robert Jensen

Robert Jensen is a professor of journalism at the University of Texas, Austin.

The preferential treatment granted to blacks through affirmative action programs is no different than the preferential treatment whites have received as a result of white privilege—the fact that many whites are granted jobs, promotions, and admission to elite universities simply because they are white. Those who complain that affirmative action programs have granted positions to blacks of mediocre talent do not realize that just as many whites of mediocre talent have advanced because of white privilege.

H ere is what white privilege sounds like:
      I'm sitting in my University of Texas office, talking to a very bright and very conservative white student about affirmative action in college admissions, which he opposes and I support.

The student says he wants a level playing field with no unearned advantages for anyone. I ask him whether he thinks that being white has advantages in the United States. Have either of us, I ask, ever benefited from being white in a world run mostly by white people? Yes, he concedes, there is something real and tangible we could call white privilege.

So, if we live in a world of white privilege—unearned white privilege—how does that affect your notion of a level playing field? I asked.

He paused for a moment and said, "That really doesn't matter."

That statement, I suggested to him, reveals the ultimate white privilege: the privilege to acknowledge that you have unearned privilege but to ignore what it means.

That exchange led me to rethink the way I talk about race and racism with students. It drove home the importance of confronting the dirty secret that we white people carry around with us every day: In a world of white privilege, some of what we have is unearned. I think much of both the fear and anger that come up around discussions of affirmative action

Reprinted from Robert Jensen, "White Privilege," *Baltimore Sun*, July 19, 1998, by permission of the author. Copyright 1998 by Robert Jensen.

has its roots in that secret. So these days, my goal is to talk openly and honestly about white supremacy and white privilege.

White privilege, like any social phenomenon, is complex. In a white supremacist culture, all white people have privilege, whether or not they are overtly racist themselves. There are general patterns, but such privilege plays out differently depending on context and other aspects of one's identity (in my case, being male gives me other kinds of privilege).

I am as white as white gets in this country. I am of northern European heritage and I was raised in North Dakota, one of the whitest states in the country. I grew up in a virtually all-white world surrounded by racism, both personal and institutional. Because I didn't live near a reservation, I didn't even have exposure to the state's only numerically significant nonwhite population, American Indians.

I have struggled to resist that racist training and the racism of my culture. I like to think I have changed, even though I routinely trip over the lingering effects of that internalized racism and the institutional racism around me. But no matter how much I "fix" myself, one thing never changes—I walk through the world with white privilege.

Automatic advantages

What does that mean? Perhaps most importantly, when I seek admission to a university, apply for a job, or hunt for an apartment, I don' t look threatening. Almost all of the people evaluating me look like me—they are white. They see in me a reflection of themselves—and in a racist world, that is an advantage. I am one of them. I am not dangerous. Even when I voice critical opinions, I am cut some slack. After all, I'm white.

My flaws also are more easily forgiven because I am white. Some complain that affirmative action has saddled the university with mediocre minority professors. I have no doubt there are minority faculty who are mediocre, though I don't know very many. As Henry Louis Gates Jr. once pointed out, if affirmative-action policies were in place for the next hundred years, it's possible that at the end of that time the university could have as many mediocre minority professors as it has mediocre white professors. That isn't meant as an insult to anyone; it's a simple observation that white privilege has meant that scores of second-rate white professors have slid through the system because their flaws were overlooked out of solidarity based on race, as well as on gender, class and ideology.

White folks have long cut other white folks a break.

Some people resist the assertions that the United States is still a bitterly racist society and that the racism has real effects on real people. But white folks have long cut other white folks a break. I know, because I am one of them. I am not a genius—as I like to say, I'm not the sharpest knife in the drawer. I have been teaching full time for six years and I've published a reasonable amount of scholarship. Some of it is the unexceptional stuff one churns out to get tenure, and some of it, I would argue, is worth reading. When I cash my paycheck, I don't feel guilty.

But I know I did not get where I am by merit alone. I benefited from, among other things, white privilege. That doesn't mean that I don't deserve my job, or that if I weren't white I would never have gotten the job. It means simply that throughout my life, I have soaked up benefits for being white.

All my life I have been hired for jobs by white people. I was accepted for graduate school by white people. And I was hired for a teaching position by the predominantly white University of Texas, headed by a white president, in a college headed by a white dean and in a department with a white chairman that at the time had one nonwhite tenured professor.

I have worked hard to get where I am, and I work hard to stay there. But to feel good about myself and my work, I do not have to believe that "merit," as defined by white people in a white country, alone got me here. I can acknowledge that in addition to all that hard work, I got a significant boost from white privilege.

Unearned success?

At one time in my life, I would not have been able to say that, because I needed to believe that my success in life was due solely to my individual talent and effort. I saw myself as the heroic American, the rugged individualist. I was so deeply seduced by the culture's mythology that I couldn't see the fear that was binding me to those myths. Like all white Americans, I was living with the fear that maybe I didn't really deserve my success, that maybe luck and privilege had more to do with it than brains and hard work. I was afraid I wasn't heroic or rugged, that I wasn't special.

I let go of some of that fear when I realized that, indeed, I wasn't special, but that I was still me. What I do well, I still can take pride in, even when I know that the rules under which I work are stacked to my benefit. Until we let go of the fiction that people have complete control over their fate—that we can will ourselves to be anything we choose—then we will live with that fear.

White privilege is not something I get to decide whether I want to keep. Every time I walk into a store at the same time as a black man and the security guard follows him and leaves me alone to shop, I am benefiting from white privilege. It is clear that I will carry this privilege with me until the day white supremacy is erased from this society.

6

Affirmative Action Harms Society

Charles T. Canady

Representative Charles T. Canady is a Florida Republican. He is the chairman of the Constitution Subcommittee of the House Judiciary Committee, and the principal sponsor of the Civil Rights Act of 1997.

By promoting a system of race-based entitlement, affirmative action is keeping America from evolving into a color-blind society where people are judged on their abilities, not the color of their skin. Affirmative action is a system of racial preferences and quotas that deny opportunity to individuals solely because they are not members of a preferred race or ethnic group. By locking deserving whites and Asians out of jobs and schools to make room for minorities with much weaker records, affirmative action exacerbates racial divisions and tensions.

On June 11, 1963, in the wake of Governor George Wallace's stand against integration at the University of Alabama, President John F. Kennedy reported to the American people on the state of civil rights in the nation. He called on Congress to pass legislation dismantling the system of segregation and encouraged lawmakers to make a commitment "to the proposition that race has no place in American life or law."

Invoking the equality of all Americans before the law, Kennedy said: "We are confronted primarily with a moral issue. It is as old as the Scriptures and it is as clear as the American Constitution. The heart of the question is whether all Americans are to be afforded equal rights and equal opportunities, whether we are going to treat our fellow Americans as we want to be treated."

The American people are now beginning a great debate over the use of race and gender preferences by federal, state, and local governments. In 1996, a majority of voters in California, including 29 percent of blacks, approved the California Civil Rights Initiative prohibiting preferential treatment in public employment, education, and contracting. In a series of cases, the Supreme Court and federal courts of appeal have made it

Adapted from Charles T. Canady, "America's Struggle for Racial Equality," a speech delivered October 1, 1997, at The Heritage Foundation, Washington, D.C.

clear that the system of preference is built on an exceedingly shaky foundation. These cases—chiefly the Adarand decision of 1995—establish that racial classifications are presumptively unconstitutional and will be permitted only in extraordinary circumstances. In 1998, Congress is likely to consider legislation to end the use of race and gender preferences by the federal government.

As we enter this debate, Kennedy's stirring words on civil rights are as important as they were in 1963. In the name of overcoming discrimination, our government for the past generation has been treating Americans of different races unequally. This is not the first time that American governments have intentionally discriminated. The institution of slavery and Jim Crow laws both violated the fundamental American tenet that "all men are created equal" and are "endowed by their Creator with certain unalienable rights." But racial preferences designed to compensate for prior discrimination are also inconsistent with our most deeply cherished principles.

Slavery was the single greatest injustice in American history. The conflict sparked by its existence and by efforts to expand it took 365,000 American lives. A system of ferocious violence that degraded human beings to the status of chattel, American slavery had at its core the belief that blacks were subhuman. It was an institution that systematically and wantonly trampled on the most basic of human relations: Husband was separated from wife, parent was separated from child. Liberty was denied to individuals solely by reason of race.

When this disgraceful chapter in our history came to an end, it left a legacy of racism that has afflicted America up to the present generation. Soon after the Civil War, that legacy found expression in the segregation statutes, also known as Jim Crow laws. Historian C. Vann Woodward describes segregation thus: "That code lent the sanction of law to a social ostracism that extended to churches and schools, to housing and jobs, to eating and drinking. Whether by law or by custom, that ostracism extended to virtually all forms of public transportation, to sports and recreations, to hospitals, orphanages, prisons, and asylums, and ultimately to funeral homes, morgues, and cemeteries."

Woodward continues, "The Jim Crow laws, unlike feudal laws, did not assign the subordinated group a fixed status in society. They were constantly pushing the Negro farther down." Woodward also documents the "total disfranchisement" of black voters in the South through the poll tax and the white primary. He quotes Edgar Gardner Murphy on the attitude of many southern whites that energized the system of segregation during the first half of the 20th century: "Its spirit is that of an all-absorbing autocracy of race, an animus of aggrandizement which makes, in the imagination of the white man, an absolute identification of the stronger race with the being of the state."

A question of dignity

The civil-rights movement of the 1950s and the early 1960s arose to combat racist laws, racist institutions, and racist practices wherever they existed. The story of that movement is a glorious chapter in the history of America. Sparked by the Supreme Court's decision in *Brown v. Board of Education* (1954), the civil-rights movement dealt a death blow to the system of segregation with the passage of the Civil Rights Act of 1964. The Voting Rights Act of 1965 soon followed, creating the basis for fully restoring the franchise to black Americans throughout the country.

The moral example of those who stood against the forces of racial injustice played a critical role in reshaping American attitudes toward race. The American people were moved by images of the terrible acts of violence and gross indignities visited on black Americans.

Moreover, the civil-rights movement embodied a fundamental message that touched the soul of the American people. It exemplified an ideal at the core of the American experience from the very beginning of our national life, an ideal that was never fully realized and sometimes tragically perverted, but always acknowledged by Americans.

The ideal of respect for the dignity of the individual was set forth in the Declaration of Independence: "[A]ll men are created equal" and are "endowed by their Creator with certain unalienable rights." At Independence Hall on the eve of the Civil War, Lincoln spoke of this ideal as "a great principle or idea" in the Declaration of Independence "which gave promise that in due time the weights should be lifted from the shoulders of all men, and that all should have an equal chance." This ideal undergirded the civil-rights movement and condemned the contradictions of America's segregated society.

This ideal has never been more eloquently expressed than by Martin Luther King Jr., who said, the "image of God . . . is universally shared in equal portions by all men. There is no graded scale of essential worth. Every human being has etched in his personality the indelible stamp of the Creator. . . . The worth of an individual does not lie in the measure of his intellect, his racial origin, or his social position. Human worth lies in relatedness to God. Whenever this is recognized, 'whiteness' and 'blackness' pass away as determinants in a relationship and 'son' and 'brother' are substituted."

King explicitly linked this religious view of man to the philosophical foundation of the United States. America's "pillars," King said, "were soundly grounded in the insights of our Judeo-Christian heritage: All men are made in the image of God; all men are brothers; all men are created equal; every man is heir to a legacy of dignity and worth; every man has rights that are neither conferred by nor derived from the state, they are God-given. What a marvelous foundation for any home! What a glorious place to inhabit!"

In light of King's personal experiences and the contradiction of sanctioning slavery and segregation in a country committed to equality, this is a remarkably optimistic view of the American experience. It is a view that propelled the civil-rights movement to great victories.

An animating principle

This understanding of the dignity of the individual found concrete expression in a legal principle that was relentlessly pursued by the early civil-rights movement. If universally adopted, this principle would fulfill the promise of American ideals. It was eloquently stated by the first Justice John Harlan in his dissent to the Supreme Court's decision in *Plessy v. Ferguson* (1896). In words that would often be cited by those seeking to overthrow the odious Jim Crow system, Harlan pronounced, "Our Constitution is color blind. . . . The law regards man as man, and takes no account of his surroundings or of his color when his civil rights as guaranteed by the Supreme law of the land are involved."

The colorblind principle articulated by Harlan was the touchstone of the American civil-rights movement until the mid-1960s. Emory law professor Andrew Kull, in his admirable history *The Color-Blind Constitution*, identifies the centrality of the colorblind principle to the movement: "The undeniable fact is that over a period of some 125 years ending only in the late 1960s, the American civil-rights movement first elaborated, then held as its unvarying political objective, a rule of law requiring the color-blind treatment of individuals."

---

*Discrimination of a most flagrant kind is now
practiced at the federal, state, and local levels.*

This fact is well illustrated by the example of Thurgood Marshall. In 1947, Marshall, representing the National Association for the Advancement of Colored People (NAACP) Legal Defense and Education Fund, in a brief for a black student denied admission to the University of Oklahoma's segregated law school, stated the colorblind principle unequivocally: "Classifications and distinctions based on race or color have no moral or legal validity in our society. They are contrary to our Constitution and laws."

Marshall's support for the colorblind principle—which he later abandoned—is vividly described by Constance Baker Motley, senior U.S. district judge for the Southern District of New York, in an account included in Tinsley Yarbrough's biography of Justice Harlan. Motley recalled her days working with Marshall at the NAACP: "Marshall had a 'Bible' to which he turned during his most depressed moments. . . . Marshall would read aloud passages from Harlan's amazing dissent. I do not believe we ever filed a major brief in the pre-*Brown* days in which a portion of that opinion was not quoted. Marshall's favorite quotation was, 'Our Constitution is color-blind.' It became our basic creed."

The principle of colorblind justice ultimately did find clear expression in the law of the United States. By passing the Civil Rights Act of 1964, Congress acted decisively against the Jim Crow system, and established a national policy against discrimination based on race and sex. It is the supreme irony of the modern civil-rights movement that this crowning achievement was soon followed by the creation of a system of preferences based first on race and then extended to gender.

The Civil Rights Act of 1964 was an unequivocal statement that Americans should be treated as individuals and not as members of racial and gender groups. Congress rejected the racism of America's past. Under the Civil Rights Act of 1964, no American would be subject to discrimination. And there was no question about what discrimination meant. Senator Hubert Humphrey of Minnesota—the chief Senate sponsor of the legislation—stated it as clearly as possible: Discrimination was any "distinction in treatment given to different individuals because of their different race."

Was this enough?

As the Civil Rights Act was being considered, some voices questioned the adequacy of the principle of colorblind justice. The Urban League's Whitney Young said that "300 years of deprivation" called for "a decade of discrimination in favor of Negro youth." James Farmer, a founder of the Congress of Racial Equality, called for "compensatory preferential treatment." Farmer said "it was impossible" for an "employer to be oblivious to color because we had all grown up in a racist society." But Roy Wilkins of the NAACP, in an encounter with Farmer, summed up the traditional view of the civil-rights movement: "I have a problem with that whole concept. What you're asking for there is not equal treatment, but special treatment to make up for the unequal treatment of the past. I think that's outside the American tradition and the country won't buy it. I don't feel at all comfortable asking for any special treatment; I just want to be treated like everyone else."

While considering the Civil Rights Act of 1964, Congress itself debated the issues of racial preferences and proportional representation. The result of that debate was the adoption of Section 703(j) of the Act, which states that nothing in Title VII of the Act "shall be interpreted to require any employer . . . to grant preferential treatment to any individual or group because of the race . . . of such individual or group" in order to maintain a racial balance. Senators Joseph Clark of Pennsylvania and Clifford Case of New Jersey, who steered that section of Title VII through the legislative process, left no doubt about Congress's intent. "[A]ny deliberate attempt to maintain a racial balance," they said at the time, "whatever such a balance may be, would involve a violation of Title VII because maintaining such a balance would require an employer to hire or refuse to hire on the basis of race. It must be emphasized that discrimination is prohibited to any individual."

Led astray

For a brief, shining moment, the principle of colorblind justice was recognized as the law of the land. But soon that principle was thrust aside to make way for a system of race-based entitlement. The critical events took place during the Nixon administration, when the so-called Philadelphia Plan was adopted. It became the prototypical program of racial preferences for federal contractors.

In February 1970, the U.S. Department of Labor issued an order that the affirmative-action programs adopted by all government contractors must include "goals and timetables to which the contractor's good faith efforts must be directed to correct . . . deficiencies" in the "utilization of minority groups." This construct of goals and timetables to ensure the proper utilization of minority groups clearly envisioned a system of proportional representation in which group identity would be a factor—often the decisive factor—in hiring decisions. Embodied in this bureaucratic verbiage was a policy requiring that distinctions in treatment be made on the basis of race.

Discrimination of a most flagrant kind is now practiced at the federal, state, and local levels. A white teacher in Piscataway, New Jersey, is fired solely on account of her race. Asian students are denied admission to state universities to make room for students of other races with much weaker records. There are more than 160 federal laws, regulations, and executive orders explicitly requiring race- and sex-based preferences.

Now, as throughout the history of preferences, the key issue in the debate is how policies of preference can be reconciled with the fundamental American tenet that "all men are created equal" and are "endowed by their Creator with certain unalienable rights."

Preferences do nothing to help develop the skills necessary for the economic and social advancement of the disadvantaged.

Evidence of racism can still be found in our country. American society is not yet colorblind. The issue for Americans today is how we can best transcend the divisions of the past. Is it through a policy of consistent nondiscrimination or through a system of preferences?

Racial preferences are frequently justified as a measure to help low-income blacks. But the evidence is compelling that the beneficiaries of preferential policies are overwhelmingly middle-class or wealthy. For the most part, the truly disadvantaged have been unable to participate in the programs that grant preferences. Furthermore, the emphasis on preferences has diverted attention from the task of addressing the root causes of black Americans' disadvantage. The lagging educational achievement of disadvantaged blacks can be ameliorated not through preferences but through structural reform of the American elementary and secondary education system. Preferences do nothing to help develop the skills necessary for the economic and social advancement of the disadvantaged.

Dressed-up discrimination

Preferences must also be judged a moral failure. Although some individuals have benefited significantly from preferences and a case can be made that preferences have enhanced the economic position of the black middle class, these gains have come at a great moral cost. Put simply, preferences discriminate. They deny opportunities to individuals solely because they are members of a nonpreferred race, gender, or ethnic group. The ambitions and aspirations, the hopes and dreams of individual Americans for themselves and for their families are trampled underfoot not for any wrongs those individuals have committed but for the sake of a bureaucratic effort to counterbalance the supposedly pervasive racism of American society. The penalty for the sins of the society at large is imposed on individuals who themselves are guilty only of being born a member of a nonpreferred group. Individual American citizens who would otherwise enjoy jobs and other opportunities are told that they must be denied in order to tilt the scales of racial justice.

Although preferences are presented as a remedial measure, they in fact create a class of innocent victims of government-imposed discrimination. In our system of justice, the burden of a remedy is imposed on those responsible for the specific harm being remedied. In the case of racial preferences, however, this remedial model breaks down. Those who benefit from the remedy need not show that they have in fact suffered any harm, and those who bear the burden of the remedy do so not because of any conduct on their part but purely because of their identity as members of nonpreferred groups. Americans of all descriptions are deprived of opportunities under the system of preferences. And some of these victims have themselves struggled to overcome a severely disadvantaged background.

The proponents of preferential policies must acknowledge the injuries done to innocent individuals. They must confront the consequences flowing daily from the system of preferences in awarding contracts, jobs, promotions, and other opportunities. Supporters of the status quo attempt to hide the reality of preferences beneath a facade of "plus factors," "goals and timetables," and other measures that are said merely to "open up access" to opportunities. Behind all these semantic games, individual Americans are denied opportunities by government simply because they are of the wrong color or sex. The names assigned to the policies that deprive them of opportunity are of little moment. What matters is that our government implements a wide range of programs with the purpose of granting favored treatment to some on the basis of their biological characteristics. How can such government-imposed distinctions be reconciled with Martin Luther King's message that whenever the image of God is recognized as universally present in mankind, "'whiteness' and 'blackness' pass away as determinants in a relationship"? The conflict is irreconcilable.

The moral failure of preferences extends beyond the injustice done to individuals who are denied opportunities because they belong to the wrong group. There are other victims of the system of preferences. The supposed beneficiaries are themselves victims.

Preferences attack the dignity of the preferred, and cast a pall of doubt over their competence and worth. Preferences send a message that those in the favored groups are deemed incapable of meeting the standards that others are required to meet. Simply because they are members of a preferred group, individuals are often deprived of the recognition and respect they have earned. The achievements gained through talent and hard work are attributed instead to the operation of the system of preferences. The abilities of the preferred are called into question not only in the eyes of society, but also in the eyes of the preferred themselves. Self-confidence erodes, standards drop, incentives to perform diminish, and pernicious stereotypes are reinforced.

Preferences attack the dignity of the preferred, and cast a pall of doubt over their competence.

All of this results from treating individuals differently on the basis of race. It is the inevitable consequence of reducing individuals to the status of racial entities. The lesson of our history as Americans is that racial distinctions are inherently cruel. There are no benign distinctions of race.

Our history—and perhaps human nature itself—renders that impossible. Although the underlying purpose of preferences was to eliminate the vestiges of racism, the mechanism of redress was fundamentally flawed. Rather than breaking down racial barriers, preferential policies continually remind Americans of racial differences.

Scarring the soul

Martin Luther King Jr. described the harm done to all Americans by the Jim Crow system: "Segregation scars the soul of both the segregator and the segregated." Similarly, every time our government prefers one individual over another on the basis of race, new scars are created, and the promise of the Declaration of Independence is deferred.

The way forward in American race relations is to embrace the vision of a colorblind legal order that was set forth 100 years ago by Justice Harlan, pursued devotedly by the civil-rights movement, articulated eloquently by President Kennedy, and enshrined in the Civil Rights Act of 1964. The way to transcend our racial divisions is to first ensure that we, as a people acting through our government, respect every person as an individual created in the image of God and honor every American as an individual whose color will never be the basis for determining his opportunities.

The original concept of affirmative action excluded any notion of preference.

This principle is consistent with the initial meaning of "affirmative action" in civil-rights law. On March 6, 1961, President Kennedy issued Executive Order 10925, establishing the President's Committee on Equal Employment Opportunity, and creating a framework for "affirmative steps" designed "to realize more fully the national policy of nondiscrimination within the executive branch of the Government." The executive order also provided that government contracts contain the following provision: "The contractor will take affirmative action to ensure that applicants are employed, and that employees are treated during employment, without regard to their race, creed, color or national origin."

The original concept of affirmative action excluded any notion of preference. Indeed, the concept of affirmative action was explicitly linked with the principle of nondiscrimination. It was to be affirmative action to ensure that individuals were treated "without regard to their race." There is no hint of group entitlement or proportional representation in the executive order. On the contrary, the exclusive focus is on the right of individuals to be treated as individuals. The "affirmative steps" were actions designed to ensure that individuals of all races would have an opportunity to compete on the basis of their individual merit.

William Van Alstyne, a law professor at Duke University, has stated it as well as anyone: "[O]ne gets beyond racism by getting beyond it now: by a complete, resolute, and credible commitment never to tolerate in one's own life—or in the life or practices of one's government—the differential treatment of other human beings by race. Indeed, that is the great lesson for government itself to teach: In all we do in life, whatever we do in life, to treat any person less well than another or to favor any more than another for being black or white or brown or red, is wrong. Let that be our fundamental law and we shall have a Constitution universally worth expounding."

The American people have embraced that commitment, and the courts have gone far toward making it our fundamental law. The only remaining question is whether the elected representatives of the people will do their part to rid our legal order of the odious distinctions of race.

7

Affirmative Action Promotes Discrimination

Lino A. Graglia

Lino A. Graglia is the A. Dalton Cross professor of law at the University of Texas, Austin.

By granting special treatment to certain groups on the basis of race, affirmative action highlights racial distinctions and exacerbates racial conflict. Affirmative action programs create an atmosphere in which blacks are taught to blame their shortcomings on whites and encouraged to believe that they are "too different" to adhere to the standards of the rest of society. Furthermore, affirmative action excuses blacks from the obligations and requirements expected of others. Racial preferences are nothing more than government-sanctioned discrimination and should be eliminated.

Insofar as it is controversial, affirmative action is a euphemism for discrimination: the granting of preference to some individuals and therefore the disfavoring of others on the basis of their race. Suggested definitions that fail to recognize this seek to evade rather than confront the only point really in contention: how is it possible to justify an official policy of classifying people by race for differential treatment?

The overwhelming objection to any race-based policy is simply that it makes one's assigned membership in a racial group, not one's individuality, the basis of governmental treatment. It leads to—indeed, it virtually compels—the organizing of racial blocs in legislatures and elsewhere in order to contend for group advantage and defend against disadvantage. It is a prescription for racial consciousness and conflict inconsistent with the maintenance of a viable multiracial society; it means abandoning hope for an integrated society and accepting the inevitability of separatism.

For most people, it is simply morally wrong for government to treat people on the basis of race. Powerful arguments should be required to overcome this obstacle, and yet the arguments offered for racial preferences are surprisingly weak. The primary argument—that preferences compensate for past unjust disadvantage—is patently invalid and obvi-

Reprinted from Lino A. Graglia, "Is Affirmative Action on the Way Out? Should It Be?" a symposium, *Commentary*, March 1998, by permission; all rights reserved.

ously uncandid. It is not possible to compensate for an injury to A, inflicted in the past by B, by granting today a benefit to C at the expense of D. Moreover, if disadvantage were the concern, evidence of disadvantage should be the criterion for compensatory treatment. Race is not a proxy for disadvantage: not all blacks and not only blacks, the primary intended beneficiaries of racial preferences, have been disadvantaged. Yet this is precisely how affirmative action operates—by racial proxy. No black applicant to the University of Texas law school, for example, has ever been denied preferential admission or financial assistance on the grounds that he is not disadvantaged or, indeed, is advantaged; it has only been necessary, and quite sufficient, that he be black. Preferential admission to selective colleges and graduate schools is an exceptionally inappropriate way of helping the children of the underclass, very few of whom, unfortunately, apply to such schools.

An inability to compete

Racial preferences, like a handicap in golf, attempt to overcome the fact that those being preferred are not competitive with others in terms of the benefit being obtained. In the case of admission to institutions of higher education, the gaps in competitiveness are typically very large indeed. For example, in 1994, the average black seventeen-year-old lagged behind the average white seventeen-year-old by 3.9 years in reading and 3.4 years in math. In 1995, the average combined SAT score of college-bound black seniors was 202 points lower than that of the average white. Perhaps most discouraging, blacks from families with annual incomes of $70,000 or more, the highest quintile, score lower than whites from families with incomes below $10,000, the lowest quintile. Admitting large numbers of blacks to selective institutions of higher education, therefore, does not involve the use of race merely to break ties or "tip the balance" in close cases, as is usually asserted by affirmative-action proponents. It involves, instead, ignoring very substantial differences in academic credentials.

[Affirmative action] is a prescription for racial consciousness and conflict inconsistent with the maintenance of a viable multiracial society.

At the graduate level, the starkness of this problem is indicated by a table in a recent issue of *The American Lawyer.* Of all law-school applicants in 1996—97, only 103 blacks and 224 Hispanics had a college grade-point average (GPA) of 3.25 and LSAT scores at or above the 83.5 percentile. Only sixteen blacks—fewer than the number admitted to Harvard law school alone in 1996–97—and 45 Hispanics were at or above the 92.3 percentile and had a 3.50 GPA. To appreciate the disparity involved, one should keep in mind that the average applicant receiving an offer from the law school of the University of California at Berkeley had an LSAT score at the 97.7 percentile and a 3.74 GPA.

The effect of racial preferences at selective colleges is virtually to guarantee that students are placed in institutions at least one level above where they would be fully competitive, a formula for frustration and resentment and the source of most of the major problems plaguing the American campus today. Inability to compete at the game being played necessarily leads to demands that the game be changed, and thus are born demands for black and ethnic studies and "multiculturalism." Such courses function to convince blacks that their academic difficulties are a result not of a lack of preparation but of white racism, and to impress upon whites their own moral shortcomings. The need to deny the lack of competitiveness on the part of members of the preferred groups leads to an insistence on political correctness, to sensitivity training, and to "hate-speech" codes.

I can personally attest from my own experience at the University of Texas that to question racial preferences—in theory, a perfectly legitimate exercise of academic freedom—is to subject oneself to charges of "racial harassment" and investigatory proceedings. Strikingly, in my case, several of my colleagues argued that anyone like me who opposes racial preferences should be disqualified from teaching any course to which "preferred" students have been assigned—an idea that, if put into practice, would bar me from teaching my basic first-year course in constitutional law.

An exaggeration of white racism

To the extent that preferences have been justified as necessary to overcome racial disadvantage, they have created an incentive to insist upon and exaggerate the pervasiveness of white racism and to contend, contrary to fact, that whites are unalterably opposed to black achievement. To the extent that these programs have been justified as providing "diversity," they have created an incentive for blacks to manifest their "differences" by seeing race at the crux of everything and by developing exceptional skill in the perception of slights. Most basically, racial preferences tend to create an expectation of a general black exemption from ordinary obligations and requirements. The thrust is toward a society in which it will be generally understood that blacks are just "too different" to be expected to conform to the rules applicable to others. This would not be a society in which blacks and whites would be likely to live together amicably.

The many arguments offered for racial preferences in admission to institutions of higher education—remedy for past injustice, diversity, the need to provide role models, and so forth—have more recently been reduced to a single one: "We can't have"—that is, it is not politically feasible to have—"all-white institutions." Of course, and in reality, American universities are in no danger of being all-white today. Asians, only 4 percent of the population, now make up 24 percent of the enrollment at Harvard and Columbia, for example, and a much higher percentage at the University of California. And even without racial preferences, blacks and Hispanics would be well represented at most public universities, if not in the numbers demanded by political correctness. The real problem is at the nation's highly selective institutions, and even those few schools would almost always have at least some black enrollment without preferences.

But where is it written that different racial or ethnic groups must appear proportionately in all institutions and activities? In American higher education, gross disproportions are already quite common. Jews, for example, at less than 3 percent of the population, make up about 40 percent of most law faculties, and Asians have come to dominate Ph.D.'s in math and science. Blacks, at 12 percent of the population, account for two-thirds of the players in professional football and four-fifths in basketball. These disproportions may conflict with some abstract egalitarian ideal, but rarely are they seen as constituting so serious a problem as to require double standards in order to produce better racial or ethnic "balances."

The California Institute of Technology, apparently operating without racial preferences, has a black enrollment of under 2 percent. To whom, if anyone, is this unacceptable? If it is unacceptable, then would it not be proper to require, at a minimum, that any steps taken to change it be openly and honestly divulged? The fact is, however, that a requirement of openness would in itself preclude many racial-preference schemes. This is not only because of the inherent moral distastefulness of preferences to most Americans, but for sound utilitarian reasons as well: think of the effect on the public of an increased awareness that racial preferences in admission to medical schools necessarily means a lower quality of medical care.

[Preferences] have created an incentive to insist upon and exaggerate the pervasiveness of white racism and to contend . . . that whites are unalterably opposed to black achievement.

After nearly 30 years of race-based public policy, many educational leaders seem simply unable to imagine our public universities operating again on the basis of race-blind admissions. Not so long ago, however, at the time of the great 1964 Civil Rights Act, the policy that was unthinkable and indefensible was a policy of racial discrimination. The Act was based on the conviction, fervently and nearly unanimously held, that all forms of racial discrimination by government are odious, immoral, and unconstitutional, to be permanently removed from American life. That conviction was correct, and we should strive to return to it.

8

Affirmative Action Harms Minority Students

Thomas Sowell

Thomas Sowell is a senior fellow at the Hoover Institution in Stanford, California.

In the past, affirmative action programs often placed good, but ill-prepared, minority students in elite schools for the sake of diversity. These students, who were capable of excelling in good colleges, were transformed into failures by being placed in high-pressure schools where only the most exemplary students can succeed. Since the elimination of affirmative action in the University of California system, minority students have been redistributed to respectable schools that better serve their capabilities.

Crucial facts have been left out in much of the hysteria about declining black enrollments at the University of California at Berkeley, in the wake of the end of affirmative action policies there. This compounds the misconceptions that existed before such policies were ended.

During the decade of the 1980s, Berkeley's rapid increase in the number of black students on campus did not translate into comparable increases in the number of blacks actually graduating. At one point, the number of black students graduating declined absolutely, while the number of blacks on campus was increasing. That was part of the high price of being more interested in racial body count than in getting people educated.

The problem was not that black students at Berkeley were "unqualified." Their test scores, for example, were above the national average. It was just that the test scores of the white and Asian students were far higher. The black students at Berkeley were perfectly qualified to be successes somewhere else, rather than being failures at Berkeley.

Now that racial double standards in admissions have been ended, many black students are in fact going elsewhere. For example, there has been an increase in the number of black applicants who meet the admissions standards at the University of California at San Diego. Is it not more

Reprinted from Thomas Sowell, "Racial Body Count Versus Education," *Conservative Chronicle*, July 23, 1997, by permission of Thomas Sowell and Creators Syndicate.

important to have these students go where they are more likely to graduate, rather than have them serve as temporary tokens on the Berkeley campus, allowing university administrators to gush about "diversity"?

Much the same story applies on other campuses across the country and for other minorities, such as Hispanic Americans.

Where group body count has been the over-riding consideration, minority students who were perfectly capable of graduating from a good college have been artificially turned into failures by being admitted to high-pressure campuses, where only students with exceptional academic backgrounds can survive.

The real issue has not been "qualified" versus "unqualified." The issue has been the systematic mismatching of minority students with the particular campuses where they have been admitted.

Once racial double standards of admission were ended, it was virtually inevitable that minority students would redistribute themselves among institutions. But the black and Hispanic students who no longer went to Berkeley did not disappear into thin air or fail to go to college at all.

UC San Diego is not chopped liver. It has respectable colleges and professional schools, and its graduates have every prospect of finding rewarding careers.

It was ironic that President Bill Clinton chose the UC San Diego campus for his speech deploring the end of affirmative action. Worse yet, the university's administration released misleading statistics, showing that the total number of minority students applying there had declined by 4 percent after affirmative action ended.

Minority students who were perfectly capable of graduating from a good college have been artificially turned into failures by being admitted to high-pressure campuses, where only students with exceptional academic backgrounds can survive.

What the same statistics also showed was that the number of minority students meeting the university's admissions standards had increased significantly, while the number of minority applicants who were clearly ineligible for admission had declined substantially, now that the double standards were ended. Black, Hispanic and American Indian applicants actually admitted to UC San Diego went up—and now they were being admitted on their qualifications.

Isn't that what we hoped for, those of us who wanted double standards ended?

Despite much hysteria over the fact that there is only one black student entering Berkeley's law school in 1997, 15 were admitted—and 14 chose to go somewhere else. These other places included Harvard, Stanford and the like, so don't shed tears over these students either.

Not only have double standards produced needless educational failures among minority students, they have polarized the races by producing great resentments among white students. It has been a policy under which both groups have lost, though in different ways—and in which the country as a whole has lost.

What has happened in California needs to happen in the other 49 states—and journalists need to start reporting the truth about it, even when the truth is not "politically correct."

9
Affirmative Action Should Be Reformed

Orlando Patterson

Orlando Patterson is a professor of sociology at Harvard and the author of The Ordeal of Integration.

Affirmative action is intended to expose African Americans to vital social networks that are critical to advancement. One problem with affirmative action, however, is that its beneficiaries tend to segregate themselves from whites. Black college students, for example, have a tendency to reside in all black student halls, and attend all black social events. Affirmative action should be reformed to better facilitate the program's original goal of fully integrating blacks into American society.

At one extreme, affirmative action is seen as a legally sanctioned remedy for past and present racial discrimination. At the other extreme, it is seen as a violation of the principle of fairness and especially of a "color-blind" society. Between these two extremes we find an evolving practice originating in a 1965 executive order. It should have been the job of the legislative arm of government to spell out both the objective and the procedures of this order, but Congress failed to do so, leaving the matter to the courts. Because the legal system is reactive rather than pro-active, it has been forced to do something it is really not qualified to do. The result has been the mishmash of contradictory rulings we now have. We are badly in need of clarity, and this is where public discourse can be useful.

Affirmative action opens vital networks

My own position is that affirmative action is a way of providing African-Americans with otherwise unavailable access to critical social networks and entry-level openings and to compensate for cultural capital deficiencies unfairly arising from the group's isolation. For, in spite of a striking decline in racism over the past decades, African-Americans, for reasons too complex to go into here, are still far too isolated.

The implications of this are made clearer if we think of America as an environment remarkably rich in cultural practices. These include the different child-rearing practices of all the many ethnic groups; the tacit regional subcultures of business, by which I mean the sorts of local practices you do not learn in business school about how really to succeed; the myriad networks of trust and influence that form the conduits of regional and national power; and so forth.

The knowledge acquired in the educational system gives an outsider access to the formal content of this environment. But this knowledge alone guarantees success only in those limited areas of the nation's economy that are knowledge- or skill-intensive, such as academia and the performing ends of the sports and entertainment industries. Elsewhere, acquiring familiarity with the life-worlds, interaction rituals, and unspoken inter-subjective agreements of success codes, and penetrating the critical networks of influence, depend on factors such as the communities in which one grows up and the friendships made in one's neighborhood, at one's schools, churches and synagogues, clubs, and workplaces, and in the course of one's daily life.

In addition to these naturally acquired ties, there are the strong contacts made through marriage. When we marry, we engage in an exchange of social and cultural dowries potentially far more valuable than gold-rimmed china. Nearly every ethnic group in the nation, including most Hispanic and Asian groups, participates in these exchanges, thereby enriching and modernizing its own subculture. The process is so powerful that it includes even groups like the Jews who have strong religious prohibitions against exogamous practices. African-Americans have been the only group isolated from these exchanges.

We cannot underestimate the impact of this exclusion. Why does a male Euro-American construction worker with a high-school degree earn more than an African-American college graduate? In a word, networks—the all-important access to friends and relatives who know about the availability of high-paying jobs even before the crew-boss. Why, in spite of their near-dominance of professional football and basketball, are so few African-Americans in management positions or in the lucrative sports-agent occupations? Racism is the simple answer, and there might be some truth to it. But it cannot be the main explanation.

A top-down strategy

Affirmative action is a middle-term solution to this problem. It leapfrogs the more long-term solution of residential and cultural integration; indeed, it promotes that solution by providing immediate access and sink-or-swim immersion into the informal and largely tacit success codes of the mainstream.

To be sure, it works only for a fraction of disadvantaged persons. Fairness requires that those who benefit from affirmative action have the basic formal knowledge of their Euro-American counterparts or the demonstrated capacity to acquire it. Affirmative action is of no use to high-school dropouts. It is a top-down strategy, aimed mainly at the most upwardly mobile members of the working and middle classes and generating a critical mass of self-perpetuating middle-class persons as well as an elite group genuinely tied into the networks of power and influence and fully acculturated in the norms and practices of the nation's ruling class.

Seen in these terms, affirmative action has been remarkably successful. The African-American middle class has grown substantially. Critics arguing that this growth began long before affirmative action commit a logical error, assuming that whatever initiated a process must account for its perpetuation. This is rarely true, beginning with original sin. (At the same time, I freely admit that the counterfactual claim—that without affirmative action, the African-American middle class would have been devastated during the conservative 1980's—is not easily proved.)

Affirmative action is a way of providing African-Americans with otherwise unavailable access to critical social networks . . . and to compensate for cultural capital deficiencies unfairly arising from the group's isolation.

Conservative social analysts can crunch opposing numbers till their computer chips melt away, but every successful African-American person, including this one, knows in his gut that, whatever his qualifications, affirmative action played a significant role in accounting for his success. To be sure, this is becoming less and less the case, but the need is still there. My own children needed it less; and I am optimistic that their own offspring will not need it at all. But we must wait till then.

What have been the costs? The frequently cited claim that affirmative action generates inefficiencies by compromising standards has never been proved. During the period of its implementation at the University of California, admissions standards rose dramatically rather than declined.

Critics of the program like to cite public-opinion polls suggesting that the great majority of Americans are opposed to affirmative action, arguing in turn that it has been extremely divisive. Defenders respond that a great deal depends on how these polls are worded: most Americans, including women and African-Americans, are opposed not to affirmative action but to quotas and to unqualified racial or gender preferences.

There is a simple way around this question. Instead of asking Americans to speculate in the abstract, one can simply ask their views about the affirmative-action programs at their own workplaces. The responses are remarkable. Over 80 percent of Euro-American workers strongly support the programs they actually know about and that directly affect them. This still does not address the issue of whether the program is in fact fair, but it does suggest that it is not undemocratic, and that a political defense of a revised version of it is possible.

Are there risks for African-Americans? Yes. There is a danger that if the program is seen as another form of entitlement, some of its beneficiaries will not push themselves to their highest potential levels of achievement. The fact that test scores overpredict the performance of African-American students bothers me.

What bothers me even more is the possibility that affirmative action may be stood on its head. Recall that my defense of the program is that it is an effective medium-term way to overcome the severe disadvantages of social and cultural isolation. But the whole point is to facilitate integration. The program is supposed to be self-canceling: its success should obviate the need for it. What, then, is one to make of the growing tendency of upwardly mobile African-Americans on the nation's campuses and in the suburbs to segregate themselves? If this tendency were to persist and spread, each generation of middle- and upper-class African-Americans would need the program. In short, it will have become an institutionalized form of bourgeois entitlement, as pernicious as subsidies to rich Euro-American farmers.

But there is an even more disturbing possibility, and worrying about it caused me a sleepless night on a recent visit to Atlanta. Atlanta prides itself on being the city "too busy to hate." (What happens when Atlantans are not busy? Never mind.) It is today a happy town. There is a large, contented African-American middle and upper class, perhaps the largest in the nation. There is also a large, happy Euro-American middle and upper class.

It should be clear to all who support affirmative action that using it as a means toward self-segregation is a gross contradiction that undercuts its justification.

Why did this make me restless? Because Atlanta remains one of the most segregated cities in the nation. A pernicious Southern compromise appears to have been worked out by the elites of the two dominant groups: Euro-American Atlantans seem to have accepted affirmative action as the price for maintaining the age-old Southern tradition of segregation. The old Jim Crow principle reigns triumphant, only now with this twist: separate but truly equal, at least among the elites. This is a perversion of affirmative action, and if this is truly where it is heading I would be ready to join forces with California's Ward Connerly in opposing it.

Mending affirmative action

But I still happen to think the program can be mended, and its original objectives achieved. Mending means, first, recognizing and being sensitive to the rights of Euro-American workers, especially the right not to have jobs they already hold threatened in any way. It also means that ethnicity can never be a substitute for critical minimal qualifications, or a substitute for competitive effort.

Second, mending means placing some long-term time limit on the program. I have proposed fifteen years, mainly because that is about how long it will take to bring the present generation of preschoolers up to college level, and I am convinced that we need at least one more educational cycle of support.

Third, I think we should sharply cut back on the number of targeted groups. It is absurd that all South Americans and even persons from

Spain, as well as East Indians, Africans, and West Indians are among potential beneficiaries. America owes these people nothing; giving them entry as immigrants is itself a privilege and gift. The program should be restricted to Native Americans, African-Americans, Puerto Ricans, native Mexican-Americans, and Euro-American women. Once a long-term time limit is established, affirmative action should be gradually transformed from an ethnic- and gender-based program to one that is class-based.

Fourth, we should specify more carefully the occupational categories and levels to which the program applies. This is going to be complicated, but it can be done. To give one example: we might want public universities to provide open access to the top 5 percent of all graduating students, but the most competitive institutions should retain the right to weed out any who fail to take advantage of the entry opportunity within the first year. We might also want to exclude all knowledge-intensive occupations. This already happens by and large, but there are borderline cases.

Finally, there should be a clear commitment from all minorities involved, especially African-Americans, that the program is predicated on the desirability and necessity of integration. Minorities unprepared to accept this condition should not benefit. How could one implement this? We could start with college campuses that bring in students on affirmative-action principles and then promptly succumb to the demand for segregated halls and events.

It should be clear to all who support affirmative action that using it as a means toward self-segregation is a gross contradiction that undercuts its justification. Affirmative action means a strong commitment to the moral and practical ideal of integration. Anything else is indefensible.

10
Affirmative Action Should Be Based on Class, Not Race

Richard D. Kahlenberg

Richard D. Kahlenberg is a fellow at the Century Foundation, a non-partisan research group that focuses on economic, social, and political institutions and issues. He is the author of The Remedy: Class, Race, and Affirmative Action.

Because a disproportionate number of minority students live in poverty, an affirmative action program based on class instead of race would be able to maintain acceptable levels of diversity within universities without resorting to racial quotas. Instead of considering test scores alone, an affirmative action program based on class would evaluate applicants in light of the disadvantages they faced. Some studies indicate that class-based affirmative action produced twice as many African American admissions to the University of California at Los Angeles than a system relying on test scores alone. Class-based affirmative action can stem falling minority enrollment, and provide equal opportunity to disadvantaged students of all races.

Ever since racial preferences were outlawed at public universities in California and Texas, the news on minority admissions at the elite public universities has been uniformly bleak. African-American, Latino, and Native-American admissions plunged among undergraduate institutions, and graduate schools saw even larger drops. Some conservatives have pointed out that the declines are proof of how deeply racial preferences had become embedded, but most Americans look at the declines with dismay: majorities don't like racial preferences, but they don't want all-white universities either.

Nathan Glazer, writing recently in the *New Republic*, argued that there is an irreconcilable conflict between principle (not judging people by skin color) and practicality (getting a racially diverse student body). In a reversal of his earlier view, Glazer now says we must resort to distasteful means in order to avoid distasteful ends (a "whiteout"). Some other con-

Reprinted from Richard D. Kahlenberg, "In Search of Fairness: A Better Way," *The Washington Monthly*, June 1998, with permission from *The Washington Monthly*. Copyright by The Washington Monthly Company, 1611 Connecticut Ave. NW, Washington, DC 20009; (202) 462-0128.

servatives fear that the dramatic decline in minority admissions will lead universities to abandon the use of standardized tests like the SAT and LSAT—and that we should stick with racial preferences as a small accommodation to racial politics rather than jettison meritocracy altogether.

But are we really faced with such Hobson's choices? What if we devised a system of admissions that was truly just, looking at academic records in the context of obstacles that individuals had overcome? It might not be fair to give Vernon Jordan's offspring a preference because they happen to be black, but why not give a leg up to disadvantaged kids of all colors, when they have done fairly well despite numerous disadvantages? A disproportionate percentage of disadvantaged students are people of color, and surely one of the central reasons minority students as a group do worse on average academically is because they face the additional obstacles that come from economic deprivation. Alas, this won't work, Glazer says: considering merit plus obstacles doesn't yield much racial diversity, "if the studies are to be believed."

Socioeconomic status

Two of the most widely discussed studies of need-based or class-based affirmative action are Harvard professor Thomas Kane's study of undergraduate admissions and University of North Carolina professor Linda Wightman's study of law school admissions. Both are pessimistic about the possibility that class-based preferences—as defined by such factors as parental income, education, and occupation—will yield much racial diversity. The problem, they both note, is that while blacks and Hispanics are disproportionately poor, poor and working-class blacks and Hispanics test worse on average than poor and working-class whites and Asians.

Kane and Wightman are correct on this limited point, but they fail to probe why this disparity exists. One important reason is that looking at standard indicators of socioeconomic status (SES)—income, occupation, and education—does not fully capture the differences, in the aggregate, between black and white economic status. Three other differences turn out to be important.

One is concentration of poverty. Sociologists know that it is a disadvantage to grow up in a poor family, but a second, independent disadvantage to grow up in neighborhoods with concentrated poverty, because such children often lack positive role models and peer influences. Because of housing discrimination, blacks are much more likely to live in concentrated poverty than whites of equal income. Indeed, one study found that in Los Angeles, affluent blacks making between $75,000 and $100,000 live in neighborhoods with higher mean poverty rates than whites with incomes in the $5,000–$10,000 range.

A second important difference between blacks and whites of the same income level has to do with differences in wealth. While median black family income is on the order of 60 percent of white income, median black net assets are 9 percent that of whites. Middle class blacks earning $45,000–$60,000 annually have a lower net worth on average than whites with incomes between $7,500 and $15,000. Family wealth affects a child's life chances in a number of ways. To take one concrete example, a study reported recently in the *Wall Street Journal* found that blacks are less likely to take LSAT preparation courses, which run as much as $1,000. For the average black, whose net worth is one-tenth the average white's, the cost of the LSAT course is the equivalent of $10,000 in white eyes.

A third important difference between blacks and whites of equal income levels has to do with family structure. The main reason it is a disadvantage to grow up in a single-parent family is that the family is likely to be low income. But studies find a second, independent disadvantage stems from growing up in a household with half the number of parents to nurture you. Again, this factor has a racial dimension: Among children under 18, 76 percent of whites but just 33 percent of blacks live with two parents.

What would happen if a university's class-based affirmative action program looked beyond just income to factors like concentration of poverty, wealth, and family structure? We now have some preliminary evidence from UCLA Law School, which implemented a race-blind, class-based affirmative action system in 1997. According to a forthcoming article by UCLA Law Professor Richard Sander in the *Journal of Legal Education*, the scheme looked at three family factors (an applicant's family income, mother's education, and father's education) and three neighborhood factors (proportion of single-parent households, proportion of families receiving welfare, and proportion of adults who had not graduated from high school). A seventh factor, family wealth, was originally included in the formula but was temporarily dropped in the final calculation for technical reasons. According to press reports, even this sophisticated system has been a failure. Jeffrey Rosen, writing in the *New Yorker*, says that UCLA's use of "seven rather Dickensian indicators of social deprivation . . . failed to produce more African-American admissions."

Why not give a leg up to disadvantaged kids of all colors, when they have done fairly well despite numerous disadvantages?

But according to Sander's study, the press reports are simply wrong. Looking at 1997's admissions, Sander told me, "Our research clearly shows that class-based affirmative action produced more than twice as many black admissions as we would have had under a system entirely driven by LSATs and grades." The effect on black enrollment was even greater. Because those African-Americans who were admitted to UCLA on test scores and grades were almost certain to have been admitted to more prestigious law schools, and were likely to have turned UCLA down, Sander found that class-based affirmative action boosted black enrollment at UCLA to 13 times what it would have been under a system of test scores and grades.

Latinos fared extremely well under the class-based affirmative action regime. Almost the entire decline in Latino admissions at UCLA in 1997 is attributable to the decline in applications—a quirk due to the fact that racial preferences were barred in California and Texas, but nowhere else in the country. Had applications not declined, Sander found, Latino admissions would have been "virtually unchanged" under the class- rather than race-based affirmative action system.

If students had been admitted purely by test scores and grades, Sander found, UCLA's enrollment would have been 2.3 percent Latino, black, and Native-American. Under UCLA's moderately aggressive use of SES, the Latino, black, and Native-American representation was 13.1 percent.

Using racial preferences, these three groups had constituted 25.1 percent of the class. Among students who scored high enough to be considered, the class-based system disproportionately benefited people of color: 14.5 percent of whites, 25.9 percent of blacks, and 30.1 percent of Latinos in the targeted test range were admitted with an SES boost.

Meanwhile, Asian-American enrollment increased by 29 percent under the new class-based system, (from 16.7 percent of the student body to 21.5 percent) and white enrollment increased by 12 percent (from 58 percent to 65 percent of the student body). The switch from race to class preferences saw an overall decline in minority enrollment, then, but it seems odd to use the term "whiteout" to refer to a class that is—after the end of racial preference—35 percent people of color.

Sander notes that UCLA was more successful than Berkeley's Boalt Hall Law School or the University of Texas Law School in maintaining some racial diversity; and he attributes the relative success to UCLA's socioeconomic program. The other law schools, he said, informally incorporated SES considerations on an individualized basis, but "they haven't articulated any sort of set of criteria that they use" or implemented preferences in a systemic way, though he notes that Boalt Hall is "actively looking at what we're doing."

Our research clearly shows that class-based affirmative action produced more than twice as many black admissions as we would have had under a system entirely driven by LSATs and grades.

Which is not to say that UCLA's own program cannot be improved in order to make it more fair, and to increase the racial dividend in the future. 1997's program did not incorporate net worth; 1998's program will. Likewise, family structure has not been part of the individual family measure, though Sander says, "We're talking about including it in the future."

Finally, UCLA chose to pursue only a moderately sized SES preference, smaller than the one provided for blacks under race-based affirmative action. With an academic index of 0–1,000 points, individuals scoring 818 were automatically admitted; the most economically disadvantaged were admitted with a 625; while under the old system blacks with scores of 550 were admitted. But arguably the economic preference should be at least as large as the preference had been for blacks, since all those benefiting from an SES boost have demonstrated an ability to overcome tangible obstacles and are likely to go much farther in life than their test scores predict. As Lani Guinier notes, Harvard found in a study of three classes that its most successful graduates 30 years later were those with low SATs and blue collar backgrounds, a group which administrators characterize as "hungry." UCLA's experience in 1997 was that the larger the SES preference, the greater the racial yield. In the 760–814 range, blacks and Latinos were admitted at twice the rate of whites; but in the 625–699 range, the multiple was eight times. According to a simulation, Sander found that using a larger socioeconomic preference—reaching down to 575—would increase black, Hispanic, and Native-American enrollment by another 46 percent above and beyond the increased representation achieved using a moderate preference. In all, the large SES boost would produce a class with seven times as many blacks, Hispanics, and Native-Americans matriculating as a system using test scores and grades alone.

Socioeconomic diversity

If UCLA's program was somewhat successful in helping to stem the decline in racial admissions, it was fabulously successful in creating greater socioeconomic diversity. In 1991, during the heyday of racial preferences at UCLA Law, Sander did a survey which found that in the national population of individuals in their twenties, those with families whose income was in excess of $200,000 were 50 times as likely to be UCLA students as individuals whose families were in poverty. These numbers track with law schools nationally, where a 1995 survey found that 41 percent of students had fathers with graduate degrees compared with 8 percent of men aged 45–64 in the general population. While law schools almost universally claim to seek socioeconomic along with racial diversity, Linda Wightman's study found that "schools are not currently placing special consideration or weight on SES factors in the admission process." After instituting the socioeconomic preference at UCLA, Sander says, "the resulting student body, as a whole, matched the American citizenry remarkably closely."

Socioeconomic diversity should, at least as much as racial diversity, enrich the academic discourse by bringing diverse experiences into the classroom. Arguably, a poor white student from a Tennessee farm might add more to the discussion in a law school class made up largely of upper-middle-class whites than a black corporate lawyer's son from Connecticut. Yet the emphasis on socioeconomic diversity is surprisingly out of fashion, Sander finds. Outside of his colleagues at UCLA, he says, "only one out of every 20 people I've talked to in the legal academy seem to attach value to the idea of economic diversity." Says Sander: "Schools that are willing to throw themselves into the fire to preserve racial effects act like class-based affirmative action is if anything a bad thing. 'Why would we want all those low-class people here?' It's very odd."

The fact that UCLA's experiment with class-based affirmative action provided substantial SES diversity and some racial diversity is a very hopeful harbinger for its use in other academic settings. For one thing, as a top 20 law school, UCLA's racial preferences had been more substantial than those employed at less selective law schools—or at most undergraduate colleges—so the racial dividend of SES preferences was harder to sustain than it will be elsewhere. Moreover, Sander says, racial declines in California and Texas public universities were "much worse" than they might otherwise have been because UCLA and others were competing for minority students against universities in 48 states (as well as against private universities in California and Texas) not subject to racial bans. Predictably, academically talented people of color shied away from California and Texas public law schools—knowing that fewer people of color were going to be admitted and not wanting to find themselves racially isolated. The number of black applications at UCLA dropped by one-third, and this drop accounts for one-third of the decline in blacks admitted, Sander says.

If the U.S. Supreme Court overturns its 1978 decision in *University of California Board of Regents v. Bakke*—so that all public and private universities are barred from using race in admissions—class-based preferences would have a dramatic effect, Sander says. "If you look at the big picture of what would happen to American legal education if you did this systemically, the racial effects would be incredible." With a racial ban, studies find that blacks are likely to shuffle down two tiers in law schools, and large numbers won't attend at all, since unlike colleges there are no nonselective law schools. Using class-based affirmative action would stem that tide, Sander says, reducing the number of blacks no longer attending law school to those who might well have failed law school or the bar anyway. "Globally, the impacts are much greater than we're talking about here [at UCLA]."

Sander's numbers suggest that even with an improved class-based affirmative action system accounting for aggregate differences between black and white poverty and giving a generous SES boost, economic status does not entirely explain the black-white test score gap and so will not result in the same level of racial diversity as the old system of racial preferences. There is no better way to ensure an entering class that is, say, 8.2 percent African-American than to count race per se. If the question is framed in terms of what provides the most efficient and ironclad way of guaranteeing a given racial representation, class is an imprecise proxy for race. But the whole point of recent court decisions and the vote in California on Proposition 209 is that people no longer accept the idea that we should mandate a given racial outcome, and fairness be damned. The fairness of racial preferences turns on whether the continuing racial gap, after factoring in economic obstacles, is due to discrimination, genetics, or culture.

As a matter of justice, one could argue, blacks should receive bonus points above and beyond any socioeconomic preference because they face discrimination not faced by whites. Granted, discrimination against an applicant's parents or grandparents in employment or housing is already captured by the economic preference for low family income and living in bad neighborhoods and attending bad schools. But what about the fact that black students themselves are more likely to be harassed by the police or by security guards in the mall or that they have difficulty getting a taxi—all because they are black? These are highly troubling forms of discrimination, and our legal system must hold discriminators accountable by, for example, punishing offending cab drivers. But it is hard to see how this form of discrimination justifies a blanket preference for all African-Americans and Latinos to Berkeley.

A more direct link might be shown if it were demonstrated that racist elementary and secondary teachers have unjustified lower expectations for black kids, which unfairly reduces their academic performance. This is a serious argument, if proven, but the proper remedy is better training of teachers. The problem with providing explicit racial preferences in university admissions to offset low expectations of K–12 teachers is that the very existence of such preferences may feed low expectations in the future. There is some evidence that the cure can promote the disease: Researchers find, for example, that the "mere mention" of affirmative action during polling can increase negative white responses about blacks generally. A final explanation might be test bias: that the SAT and LSAT are culturally biased and do not demonstrate the innate ability of students. The claim is certainly true—the tests are culture-bound—but it is highly important that all students be able to master mainstream American culture. As Alexander Bickel wrote: "Culture in the larger sense is what universities aim to transmit and what students must work and achieve in."

A system of admissions that looks at talent plus obstacles seems to provide the best approximation of equal opportunity.

In any event, the Supreme Court does not allow universities to give preferences to African-Americans on the presumption of societal discrimination. In practice, remedial preferences are normally available only if an individual applicant documents specific ways in which discrimination has made her academic record unpredictive of her long-term potential. Where such showings can be made, these individualized preferences based on racial discrimination (as opposed to race) are in my view fully justified; but that is quite different from adding large bonus points based on skin color across the board.

On the other extreme, there is the genetic explanation, an ugly theory that rears its head periodically, but has been thoroughly discredited on each occasion. It may be that some conservatives embrace racial preference precisely because they suspect that there are deep intractable genetic differences between racial groups, and preferences are the only way to keep the peace. Nathan Glazer, for example, responded to the argument made in *The Bell Curve* not by disputing its accuracy but by asking, "whether the untruth is not better for American society than the truth." At bottom, those who say class-based affirmative action won't produce additional racial diversity—no matter how fair—are too pessimistic about the abilities of black people.

A third possibility for the continuing test gap is cultural. As proponents of diversity themselves point out, race and ethnicity are rough proxies for culture, and cultural differences can be meaningful and significant. As a group, Asian-Americans are outperforming whites academically and constitute 38.3 percent of those admitted to Berkeley under the new race-blind admissions process, even though they make up only one-ninth of the California population. Obviously, the fact that whites perform more poorly than Asian-Americans cannot be pinned on discrimination, and culture plays a significant role. This cultural factor is more mutable than genetics, but less responsive to public policy than discrimination.

Overcoming obstacles

In the end, then, a system of admissions that looks at talent plus obstacles seems to provide the best approximation of equal opportunity. On the means side, it is likely to comport with political, legal, and moral views of fairness. People accept the notion that the poor face obstacles, and are supportive of the progressive income tax but would likely balk at a higher marginal tax rate for whites than blacks. According to a December 1997 *New York Times* poll, Americans reject racial preferences 52–35 percent but in the event of their demise, support preferences for the poor by 53–37 percent. On the result side, class-based affirmative action will produce more racial diversity than straight reliance on tests and grades; less racial diversity than a reliance on racial preference; and more socioeconomic diversity than either approach. Rather than covering up an unjustified reliance on test scores (that ignores background unfairness) with cosmetic racial preferences, we should harness the desire for inclusion to ensure that the entire system is more just.

The experience at UCLA shows that while there is some tension between justice and ethnic proportionality, between genuine equal opportunity and equal group results, there is not an ironclad contradiction, as the racial pessimists have been insisting. Fairness—genuinely and aggressively sought after—is compatible with, indeed helps secure, important measures of racial and economic diversity.

Organizations to Contact

The editors have compiled the following list of organizations concerned with the issues debated in this book. The descriptions are derived from materials provided by the organizations. All have publications or information available for interested readers. The list was compiled on the date of publication of the present volume; the information provided here may change. Be aware that many organizations take several weeks or longer to respond to inquiries, so allow as much time as possible.

Adversity.Net
802 Argyle Rd., Silver Spring, MD 20901
(301) 588-0778 • fax: (301) 589-0324
e-mail: editor@adversity.net • website: http://www.adversity.net

Adversity.Net opposes racial discrimination against anyone, including racial discrimination against nonminorities. It publishes fact sheets and case histories regarding reverse discrimination.

American Civil Liberties Union (ACLU)
125 Broad St., 18th Fl., New York, NY 10004
(212) 549-2500 • fax: (212) 549-2646
website: http://www.aclu.org

The ACLU is a national organization that works to defend Americans' civil rights as guaranteed by the U.S. Constitution. It works to establish equality before the law, regardless of race, color, sexual orientation, or national origin. The ACLU publishes and distributes policy statements, pamphlets, and the semiannual newsletter *Civil Liberties Alert*.

Canadian Human Rights Commission (CHRC)
344 Slater St., 8th Fl., Ottawa, ON K1A 1E1 CANADA
(613) 996-5211 • fax: (613) 996-9661
e-mail: info.com@chrc-ccdp.ca • website: http://www.chrc-ccdp.ca

Established in 1978, the Canadian Human Rights Commission educates Canadians on human rights issues, provides effective and timely means for resolving individual complaints, and helps reduce barriers to equality in employment and access to services. It publishes the quarterly *Equality Newsletter*, employer and employee workplace guides, and information sheets.

Cato Institute
1000 Massachusetts Ave. NW, Washington, DC 20001-5403
(202) 842-0200 • fax: (202) 842-3490
e-mail: cato@cato.org • website: http://www.cato.org

The Cato Institute is a libertarian public policy research foundation dedicated to limiting the control of government and protecting individual liberties. It offers numerous publications on public policy issues, including the triennial *Cato Journal*, the bimonthly newsletter *Cato Policy Report*, and the quarterly magazine *Regulation*.

Center for Equal Opportunity (CEO)
815 15th St. NW, Suite 928, Washington, DC 20005
(202) 639-0803 • fax: (202) 639-0827
e-mail: comment@ceousa.org • website: http://www.ceousa.org

The Center for Equal Opportunity is the only think tank devoted exclusively to the promotion of colorblind equal opportunity and racial harmony. CEO sponsors conferences, supports research, and publishes policy briefs on issues related to race, ethnicity, assimilation, and public policy. *The Tragedy of Civil Rights: How Equal Opportunity Became Equal Results* and *Not a Close Question: Preferences in University Admissions* are among its titles.

The Claremont Institute
250 W. 1st St., Suite 330, Claremont, CA 91711
(909) 621-6825 • fax: (909) 626-6824
e-mail: info@claremont.org • website: http://www.claremont.org

The Claremont Institute supports limited government and opposes affirmative action initiatives. Its publications include *America's Passion for Fairness*, *The Affirmative Action Trainwreck: Why "Mend It, Don't End It" Won't Work*, and *Equal Opportunity Denied: Nine Case Studies in Reverse Discrimination*.

The Heritage Foundation
214 Massachusetts Ave. NE, Washington, DC 20002-4999
(202) 546-4400 • (800) 544-4843 • fax: (202) 544-6979
e-mail: pubs@heritage.org • website: http://www.heritage.org

The foundation is a conservative public policy research institute dedicated to free-market principles, individual liberty, and limited government. It opposes affirmative action for women and minorities and believes the private sector, not government, should be relied upon to ease social problems and to improve the status of women and minorities. The foundation publishes the periodic *Backgrounder* and the quarterly *Policy Review* as well as numerous monographs, books, and papers on public policy issues.

Independent Women's Forum (IWF)
PO Box 3058, Arlington, VA 22203-0058
(703) 558-4991 • (800) 224-6000 • fax: (703) 558-4994
e-mail: info@iwf.org • website: http://www.iwf.org

The Independent Women's Forum is a nonprofit, nonpartisan organization founded by women to foster public education and debate about legal, social, and economic policies affecting women and families. IWF is committed to policies that promote individual responsibility, limited government, and economic opportunity. It publishes *The Women's Quarterly* journal, policy statements, and press releases which include *Anita Blair: IWF Says No to New ERA* and *Civil Rights and Affirmative Action*.

Institute for Justice
1717 Pennsylvania Ave. NW, Suite 200, Washington, DC 20006
(202) 955-1300 • fax: (202) 955-1329
e-mail: general@ij.org • website: http://www.ij.org

The Institute for Justice is a libertarian public interest law firm that pursues cutting-edge litigation on behalf of individuals whose civil rights are denied by the state. It publishes the bimonthly *Liberty and Law* newsletter and the reports *Putting the California Civil Rights Initiative in Context* and *State of the Supreme Court: The Justices' Records on Civil and Economic Liberties.*

Leadership Conference on Civil Rights (LCCR)
1629 K St. NW, Suite 1010, Washington, DC 20006
(202) 466-3311 • fax: (202) 466-3435
e-mail: comlccr@civilrights.org • website: http://www.civilrights.org

The Leadership Conference on Civil Rights is the nation's oldest, largest, and most diverse coalition of organizations committed to the protection of civil and human rights in the United States. It represents people of color, women, labor unions, persons with disabilities, older Americans, major religious groups, gays and lesbians, and civil liberties and human rights groups.

National Association for the Advancement of Colored People (NAACP)
1025 Vermont Ave. NW, Suite 1120, Washington, DC 20005
(202) 638-2269
e-mail: hshelton@naacp.net.org • website: http://www.naacp.org

The NAACP is the oldest and largest civil rights organization in the United States. Its principal objectives are to achieve equal rights and to eliminate racial prejudice by removing racial discrimination in housing, employment, voting, education, the courts, and business. The NAACP publishes a variety of newsletters, books, and pamphlets as well as the magazine *Crisis.*

Pacific Research Institute for Public Policy (PRIPP)
755 Sansome St., Suite 450, San Francisco, CA 94111
(415) 989-0833 • fax: (415) 989-2411
website: http://www.pacificresearch.org

The Pacific Research Institute for Public Policy promotes the principles of individual freedom and personal responsibility. The Institute believes these principles are best encouraged through policies that emphasize a free economy, private initiative, and limited government. Its publications include the monthly newsletter *Impact* and the book *Unfinished Business: A Civil Rights Strategy for America's Third Century.*

U.S. Equal Employment Opportunity Commission (EEOC)
1801 L St. NW, Washington, DC 20507
(202) 663-4900
website: http://www.eeoc.gov

The mission of the EEOC is to promote equal opportunity in employment through administrative and judicial enforcement of the federal civil rights laws and through education and technical assistance. It publishes numerous press releases pertaining to affirmative action.

Wider Opportunities for Women (WOW)
815 15th St. NW, Suite 916, Washington, DC 20005
(202) 638-3143 • fax: (202) 638-4885
e-mail: info@w-o-w.org • website: http://www.w-o-w.org

WOW works to expand employment opportunities for women by overcoming sex-stereotypic education and training, work segregation, and discrimination in employment practices and wages. In addition to pamphlets and fact sheets, WOW publishes the quarterly newsletter, *Women at Work.*

Bibliography

Books

Barbara Bergmann · *In Defense of Affirmative Action.* New York: BasicBooks, 1996.

Clint Bolick · *The Affirmative Action Fraud: Can We Restore the American Civil Rights Vision?* Washington, DC: Cato Institute, 1996.

Thomas D. Boston · *Affirmative Action and Black Entrepreneurship.* New York: Routledge, 1999.

William G. Bowen and Derek Curtis Bok · *The Shape of the River: Long-Term Consequences of Considering Race in College and University Admissions.* Princeton, NJ: Princeton University Press, 1998.

Lydia Chavez · *The Bind: California's Battle to End Affirmative Action.* Berkeley: University of California Press, 1998.

George E. Curry and Cornel West, eds. · *The Affirmative Action Debate.* Reading, MA: Perseus, 1996.

Walter Feinberg · *On Higher Ground: Education and the Case for Affirmative Action.* New York: Teachers College Press, 1997.

Mildred Garcia, ed. · *Affirmative Action's Testament of Hope: Strategies for a New Era in Higher Education.* Albany: State University of New York Press, 1997.

Richard D. Kahlenberg · *The Remedy: Class, Race, and Affirmative Action.* New York: HarperCollins, 1997.

Darrien A. McWhirter · *The End of Affirmative Action: Where Do We Go from Here?* Secaucus, NJ: Birch Lane, 1996.

Stephan Thernstrom and Abigail Thernstrom · *America in Black and White: One Nation, Indivisible.* New York: Touchstone Books, 1999.

Susan Welch and John Gruhl · *Affirmative Action and Minority Enrollments in Medical and Law Schools.* Ann Arbor: University of Michigan Press, 1998.

Bob Zelnick · *Backfire: A Reporter's Look at Affirmative Action.* Washington, DC: Regnery, 1996.

Periodicals

Julian E. Barnes · "A Surprising Turn on Minority Enrollments," *U.S. News & World Report,* December 9, 1997.

William G. Bowen, Derek Curtis Bok, and Glenda Burkhart · "A Report Card on Diversity: Lessons for Business from Higher Education," *Harvard Business Review,* January/February 1999.

Roger Clegg "Beyond Quotas," *Policy Review*, May/June 1998.

Kimberle Williams "Fighting the Post-Affirmative Action War," *Essence*, July
Crenshaw 1998.

David Gergen "A Study in Black and White," *U.S. News & World Report*,
October 12, 1998.

Nicholas deB. "Not Colorblind: Just Blind," *New York Times Magazine*,
Katzenbach and February 22, 1998.
Burke Marshall

John Leo "Don't Get Hysterical," *U.S. News & World Report*, April
27, 1998.

Glenn C. Loury "Color-Blinded," *New Republic*, August 17, 1998.

Orlando Patterson "Affirmative Action: Opening Up Workplace Networks
to Afro-Americans," *Brookings Review*, Spring 1998.

Robert J. Samuelson "Poisonous Symbolism," *Newsweek*, July 28, 1997.

Nina H. Shokraii "Raising the Bar: Minority Pupils Excel the Old-
Fashioned Way," *Policy Review*, March/April 1996.

Peter Skerry "The Affirmative Action Paradox," *Society*, October 1998.

Thomas Sowell "Drive a Stake Through It," *Forbes*, August 26, 1996.

Shelby Steele "How Liberals Debase Black Achievement," *Policy Review*,
November/December 1998.

Stephan Thernstrom "Racial Preferences: What We Now Know," *Commentary*,
and Abigail February 1999.
Thernstrom

Adrian Wooldridge "A True Test: In Defense of the SAT," *New Republic*, June
15, 1998.

Index

DATE DUE
